Towards Teaching Philosophy

Towards Teaching Philosophy

STEVEN M. CAHN

RESOURCE *Publications* · Eugene, Oregon

TOWARDS TEACHING PHILOSOPHY

Resource Publications
An Imprint of Wipf and Stock Publishers
199 W. 8th Ave., Suite 3
Eugene, OR 97401

www.wipfandstock.com

PAPERBACK ISBN: 979-8-3852-6126-0
HARDCOVER ISBN: 979-8-3852-6127-7
EBOOK ISBN: 979-8-3852-6128-4

VERSION NUMBER 02/13/26

To my wife,
Marilyn Ross, MD

Contents

Acknowledgments

THIS BOOK INCLUDES MATERIAL adapted from my earlier work *Teaching Philosophy: A Guide*, published by Routledge, as well as from revisions of posts I contributed to the Blog of the American Philosophical Association. I am grateful to Routledge and the American Philosophical Association, respectively, for the permissions they granted.

My thanks to Wipf and Stock Publishers for continuing support of my work and especially to Savanah N. Landerholm for her expert typesetting and design.

I have benefitted greatly from suggestions, literary and otherwise, offered by my brother, Victor L. Cahn, playwright, critic, and professor emeritus of English at Skidmore College. I am also indebted to Dr. Mary Ann McHugh, instructor in the Hugh Downs School of Human Communication at Arizona State University, for her elegant polishing of the entire manuscript. To my wife, I owe more than I would try to express.

Introduction

One approach to exploring the teaching of philosophy is to focus on the nature of philosophical inquiry, then consider how it can be taught. Another way, which I have chosen, is to focus on the nature of teaching, then consider how it applies to philosophy.

This strategy rests on my view that the essentials of effective instruction remain the same, regardless of the subject or level. Show me an effective teacher of mathematics, history, or literature, whether in college or pre-college, and I'll show you someone who with specialist study and a penchant for the field could become an effective teacher of philosophy. Likewise, show me a boring teacher of philosophy and I'll show you someone who would likely be equally tiresome presenting any subject to any audience.

Just as various performers can interpret the same piece of music in vastly different, although equally effective ways, so a philosophical text or issue can be approached using a variety of successful methods. Trying to enumerate them all would be a Sisyphean task. But just as a musician's performance can be unsatisfactory, so can a teacher's.

No matter how strong your philosophical abilities, if you don't attend to your teaching, then you're unlikely to succeed in the classroom. And those with the bad luck to be your students are apt to waste their time, money, and energy.

Furthermore, our democratic society will lose an opportunity to provide some of its citizens with a key component of liberal education: the ability to scrutinize the fundamental principles of thought and action. The path to acquiring such intellectual perspective lies in the study of those subtle analyses and grand visions that constitute philosophy. No other subject affords a stronger defense against intimidation by dogmatism while simultaneously providing a framework for the operation of intelligence.

But how to avoid pedagogical failure? For nearly a decade I offered doctoral students in the Philosophy Program at the Graduate Center of the City University of New York a fourteen-week, credit-bearing practicum titled "Teaching Philosophy." The goal was to prepare new or inexperienced teachers to offer effective instruction for undergraduates. While some class time was spent exploring pedagogic principles and moral obligations, as well as strategies for testing and grading, most of the hours were devoted to practice. Each of the approximately fifteen students gave a series of five-to-ten minute presentations intended for an introductory class, after which the speaker received immediate feedback, first from the other students, then from me.[1]

The results were dramatic. Indeed, at the undergraduate institutions where the students went to teach, department chairs reported how well our students were performing and urged continued efforts to enhance the pedagogical skills of future instructors.

Sad to say, however, the majority of members in our doctoral program were focused on increasing research productivity and believed time spent on improving teaching could be more effectively used trying to prepare articles for publication. Hence, when I retired, the course was abandoned, and as a result, the undergraduate department chairs began to criticize our students' inadequate performance in the classroom. Not surprisingly, such complaints went unheeded.

In this volume I have attempted to capture the essence of that course so that its central insights might be widely available. I recognize, of course, that no book can replace intensive practice with the guidance of a committed instructor and insightful comments from fellow students. Nevertheless, I hope my suggestions will prove useful.

1. A fuller account of the course can be found in Steven M. Cahn, *Professors as Teachers* (Eugene, OR: Wipf and Stock Publishers, 2022), 16–20.

I should add that here is not the place to score points in philosophical or meta-philosophical debates nor express support for any particular curricular or technological innovations. My focus, rather, is on identifying and analyzing the fundamental elements of success in teaching philosophy.

I

Caring About Students

ONCE AT A MEETING of the American Philosophical Association, I passed a group of graduate students who were responding enthusiastically as one described a position for which he had just been interviewed. "It's a great job," he told his friends. "There's very little teaching, and I'll have plenty of time for my work." I wish someone had informed him that teaching *was* his work.

He might have replied, however, that many highly regarded professors only grudgingly give time or attention to the classroom. Instead, they concentrate on their own scholarship.

In that regard, consider a professor I once knew who enjoyed a strong reputation for his research. Yet he regularly cancelled classes. He arrived late when he did attend and was often unprepared. He constructed no examinations so that he would have none to correct. In each course, he assigned one term paper. If he liked the first few pages, he gave the student an A for the course. If he wasn't impressed, he gave a B. Those who didn't submit a paper received a C. This grading system avoided most complaints, although occasionally a student who had received a B would grumble. The matter would be settled quickly, though, by the instructor's graciously changing the B to an A.

Surely, this celebrated scholar was unethical. He was akin to a corrupt executive or a crooked judge. He held an honorable title but abused the responsibilities of his position.

Fortunately, more professors than might be supposed act wholly otherwise. They are deeply concerned whether their students become interested in the subject, grasp assigned readings, understand explanations, and find to be reasonable assignments, examinations, and grades.

Why do these instructors care? They realize that teaching has a moral dimension because students can be helped or harmed by their educational experience. Thus, conscientious faculty take seriously pedagogic duties.

Now let's return to a variation on the story with which I began. Suppose you go to a doctor's office and overhear the physicians discussing with zest the possibility that one of them might be fortunate enough to obtain a laboratory position that would not involve seeing any patients. As you listen, you realize that these practitioners are concerned primarily with their own research, not with your personal medical problems. In such circumstances, most of us would seek doctors who are more eager to provide help. Likewise, students respond negatively to any professor who by word or deed reflects the attitude that teaching is merely a distraction from the essence of the academic enterprise.

Nevertheless, a colleague might ask skeptically, "Why should I put effort into classes when doing so doesn't advance my career?" Here is a version of the familiar challenge "Why should I be moral?" Whatever the reply, if a professor doesn't care about students, then they are the losers.

2

Teaching All the Students

YEARS AGO, THE DEPARTMENT of which I was then a member invited to campus a promising candidate for a faculty position. He had been highly recommended in part on his purported pedagogical skills, but after listening to him present a convoluted talk, I had doubts. Later, as he recounted his success in teaching introductory philosophy, I asked him to estimate the percentage of students in the class who understood his lectures. "Definitely half," he replied proudly. When I inquired about the other half, he answered that they were not philosophically sophisticated enough to follow the arguments. No wonder, given my department's commitment to excellence in teaching, he was not offered a position.

We all recognize that some students are stronger than others, and often the temptation is to focus on the standouts. The aim of teaching, however, is not to captivate instructors but to enlighten students. And although some are difficult to reach, all who are trying to learn should be offered help. Remember, every student is registered for the course and deserves attention. Furthermore, most have the necessary ability to succeed, assuming their instructor is capable and cares about their progress.

Concern for all students is compatible with reaching out to the strongest, perhaps by offering them in-class challenges or extra-credit assignments. In truth, though, the talented do not need more help than others. Do you suppose Plato was worried whether he could keep Aristotle's attention?

While few professors underestimate how much their students are learning, many instructors overestimate. They are dismayed when an examination paper displays egregious misunderstanding, and they are apt to disparage students whose work contains simple errors. A likely explanation for the phenomenon, however, is that the instruction was inadequate. A professor dissatisfied with the performance of students may take refuge in supposing that the material lies beyond their grasp, but as Tamar Szabó Gendler, then dean of the Faculty of Arts and Sciences at Yale University, once remarked to me, any subject can be explained successfully if you know how.

The challenge of effective teaching is to reach more than the students who come to class with enthusiasm and continually raise their hands to participate. Rather, the key is whether you can appeal to students who arrive with little interest and seemingly limited talents: Can you excite these students about the material and enhance their knowledge and skills?

Admittedly, doing so is difficult. Yet good teachers sometimes succeed, and great teachers often do. Granted, even the finest instructors fail occasionally, but in that case, they are likely to express dissatisfaction not with their students but with themselves.

At an interview, when candidates are asked about the extent of their success in the classroom, I have little confidence in anyone who replies, "I don't think too much about teaching, but mine's okay." Rather, I hope to hear, "I believe I reach the students, but I'm always trying to improve." The most unsatisfying answer, which I have heard too often, is "I work well with good students." In that case, I am always tempted to respond, "Who doesn't?"

3

A Teacher's Responsibilities

A FORMER COLLEAGUE OF mine once told me that her class in the history of modern philosophy was jumping from Leibniz to Kant, omitting the empiricists Locke, Berkeley, and Hume. When I asked why she was proceeding so oddly, she replied that she had asked her class to vote, and they had preferred not to study the empiricists.

The truth was that this instructor, knowing little about the empiricists, wanted to omit them but not be blamed for such an obvious gap. She tried to absolve herself of responsibility by describing the empiricists negatively, then asking her students for their preference. She persuaded them easily because as far as they knew, Locke, Berkeley, and Hume might have been the outfield for the 1918 Boston Red Sox.

Teachers cannot avoid responsibility for guiding the learning process. They should be expected to know which material is to be studied and in what order it is best presented. They should also understand how a student can proceed most productively, what constitutes individual progress, and when someone has achieved it.

Suppose you enroll in an introductory course in chess where your instructor begins by inquiring whether the class would prefer to learn first how rooks move or when castling is permitted. Such a question would be pointless, for a reasonable answer depends on some knowledge of chess, and if you already had that, you wouldn't be in a course for beginners.

As teachers are appropriately held responsible for what occurs in the classroom, so with responsibility goes authority. We speak not only of authority as power but also of an authority, that is, an expert. The two concepts are related, for the responsibilities that entail the exercise of authority or power are typically assigned to individuals by virtue of their presumed authority or expertise.

Such is the case with teachers, for their superior knowledge justifies their being assigned pedagogic responsibilities. After all, if teachers understand a subject no better than their students, why should students be charged tuition while teachers receive paychecks? I have heard teachers minimize their own importance and emphasize how much they learned from their students, but I have yet to hear a single professor offer to exchange an instructor's salary for a student's bill.

To recognize a teacher's authority, however, is not to suggest that teachers should act in an authoritarian manner. The appropriate relationship is that of guide, not god.

Guides are expected to be familiar with the area through which they lead, pointing out highlights and warning of dangers. They are to blame if you follow their instructions but miss important sites or fall victim to a peril that should have been anticipated. The guide who responds to charges of incompetence by blaming the visitors' lack of knowledge is not relieved of responsibility.

An effective guide not only knows the subject but also knows how to explain it so that learners acquire both understanding and appreciation. No matter how knowledgeable or passionate a guide may be, if that knowledge or passion is not transferred, then the guide has not succeeded.

You may find unsettling the idea that someone who knows less about a subject than you may teach it more successfully. Yet that principle is widely recognized. Do you want to learn how to swim? An Olympic champion is not necessarily an ideal person to consult. Do you want to learn to play the piano? The winner of a major international piano competition is not necessarily suited to the task.

Those who excel in a field may struggle to put themselves in the place of a beginner and may have no desire to try. Yet realizing how the subject appears to a novice is essential in grasping how to present material to those who have no understanding of it. If you do not find fulfillment in guiding those who are lost, then your obligations as a teacher will prove onerous and your students will be shortchanged.

4

How Teachers Succeed

What do successful teachers have in common that others lack? The answer is not that they know the subject especially well, because, as we have seen, knowing a subject and knowing how to teach it effectively are quite different. Rather, those who succeed have mastered three key elements.

The first is commonly referred to as *motivation*. Without it, a class stagnates. After all, how long will you watch a movie that does nothing to capture your attention? Or read a novel that begins with a situation of no interest? The slower the start, the more difficult to generate enthusiasm. At best, the audience allows you a few minutes without much action. The same with teaching.

Consider the openings of the following two lectures, delivered in the years 1970 and 1969 as the Presidential Addresses of the Eastern Division meeting of the American Philosophical Association. In 1970, the speaker was the eminent American philosopher Wilfrid Sellars, who taught at the University of Pittsburgh. He began as follows:

> The quotation which I have taken as my text occurs in the opening paragraphs of the Paralogisms of Pure Reason in which Kant undertakes a critique of what he calls 'Rational Psychology.' The paragraphs are common to the two editions of the *Critique of Pure Reason*, and the

> formulations they contain may be presumed to have continued to satisfy him—at least as introductory remarks.[1]

If your interest in reading further is minimal, many in the large audience shared that attitude, for although the subject matter was relevant to Kant scholars, not one word Sellars offered motivated his other listeners.

What could he have done instead?

One answer is found in the address given a year earlier by the renowned British philosopher Stuart Hampshire, then teaching at Princeton University. He, too, wished to give an exposition of a text but offered a far more provocative opening:

> I want to speak today about a philosophy of mind to which I will not at first assign an identity or date, except that its author could not have lived and worked before 1600. He is modern, in the sense that he thinks principally about the future applications of the physical sciences to the study of personality. As I speak, I hope that it will not at first be too easy for you to tell whether or not he is our contemporary, whether indeed he is not present in this room. I attempt this reconstruction as a way of praising a philosopher who has not, I think, been at all justly interpreted so far.[2]

Hampshire's withholding the name of the author was a brilliant stroke because members of the audience were immediately curious as to whom he was referring. As they looked around, wondering if the subject was there, they listened carefully, treating Hampshire's every sentence as a clue. Finally, a few minutes from his conclusion, Hampshire revealed that the author in question was Spinoza and ended by quoting the passage from Spinoza's *Ethics* that had been the unspoken focus: "The human mind not only perceives the affections of the human body, but also the idea of these affections" (I:22).

1. *Proceedings and Addresses of the American Philosophical Association*, vol. XLIV (September, 1971), 5.

2. *Proceedings and Addresses of the American Philosophical Association*, vol. XLIII (September, 1970), 5.

Had Hampshire begun by quoting the text he intended to discuss, the philosophical substance would have been unchanged, but doing so would have been a pedagogical disappointment, for few would have listened so attentively. But by making his talk a puzzle, Hampshire captivated his audience, and, having been present myself, I can testify that the quiet in the hall was striking.

Hampshire's talk was no richer philosophically than that of Sellars'. Pedagogically speaking, though, their two lectures were of vastly different quality.

Now let me ask: Do you admire Hampshire's strategy, or do you find it a distraction that could have been eliminated with no loss of philosophical content? If the latter, then, however strong your philosophical skills, you're not thinking as a teacher, and your performance in the classroom is apt to leave your students uninterested and unresponsive. On the other hand, if you appreciate Hampshire's approach, then I hope you will try to develop your own motivational devices that you can use each time you teach.

Walking into class and beginning with "Let's turn to page 179" will not generate electricity. A challenging puzzle or stimulating thesis is far more likely to capture the attention of your listeners.

Here's an example I offer not because of its profundity but simply because I found it worked with students. (I should add that while my own success in the classroom does not equal that achieved by some others I have known, I take second place to no one in my admiration for the performance of those I consider great teachers.)[3] In introductory philosophy, I usually included Mill's discussion of the case for free thought and discussion in chapter two of *On Liberty*. Although I assigned the relevant pages for preparatory reading, I didn't begin the class by referring to Mill or his book. Rather, I asked the class to suppose that upon entering the building they had seen a table where passersby were invited to sign a letter addressed to the administration, demanding that an invited speaker not be allowed to appear due to a well-documented record of having expressed racist and sexist sentiments.

3. See *Bronx Socrates: Portrait of a Legendary Teacher*, ed. Steven M. Cahn (Eugene, OR: Wipf and Stock Publishers, 2024).

"Would you sign?" I inquired. Most were sure they would, and the few holdouts quickly lost confidence in their position as others accused them of insensitivity to those who had been victims of prejudice. At that point I asked: Would John Stuart Mill sign the petition? Suddenly, the students recognized the significance of Mill's defense of free expression and agreed that Mill would refuse to sign. Then I asked students to explain Mill's position, and the discussion proceeded apace.

What such a motivational device does is make apparent the connections between seemingly esoteric material and the students' own sphere of experience, so that the subject becomes their personal concern. I know of no formula for developing effective motivational devices, which is one reason why teaching is an art. Even a weak attempt to motivate, however, is better than none.

Each time you enter a classroom you should have thought about how you plan to present the material so that students will become interested. You may not always find an effective means of achieving your goal, but when you do, you can add to your repertoire of motivational techniques.

Even with a motivated student, though, a successful teacher needs to know how to take advantage of such interest. A key element is organization, presenting material in a sequence that promotes understanding.

To recognize the difficulty of doing so, imagine trying to explain baseball to a person unfamiliar with the sport. Where would you begin? With the role of the pitcher and catcher? How about the calling of balls and strikes? Or the location of the bases, the means of scoring runs, or the ways outs can be made? The fundamental difficulty is that all these starting points presume knowledge of some of the others. How, then, can you break the cycle of intertwining concepts and render the subject both accessible and engaging?

Consider the following effort: "In playing baseball you try to score runs. Only the team to whom the ball is pitched can score. You run around the bases and try to avoid outs. Three strikes and you're out. The game has nine innings." This attempt is a failure.

Not that any of the statements is false. Each is true yet not only disconnected from the previous ones but also presuming knowledge the listener doesn't possess.

The first statement refers to "runs," but the learner hasn't been told how a run is scored. The second statement refers to a ball being "pitched," but the role of the pitcher hasn't been explained. The remaining statements refer to "bases," "strikes," and "outs," but none of these terms has been put in context. In short, if you don't understand baseball, you won't learn much from these remarks. Thus, an explanation can be factual yet pedagogically unsuccessful due to a lack of effective organization. Incidentally, one strategy that my brother, an acclaimed teacher, suggested is to start by presenting the diagram of a baseball field, indicating fair and foul territory, the location of the bases, the batter's potential route around them, and the placement of the pitcher, catcher, and fielders; with that information, the concepts of outs, runs, balls and strikes, and innings can be rendered comprehensible.

Let me next offer a philosophical example of the need for organization. Suppose you are planning to discuss Robert Nozick's concept of knowledge as tracking the truth. Unless you first explain the traditional three-part definition of knowledge, then ensure that everyone understands the challenge to that definition presented by the counterexamples associated with Edmund Gettier, trying to discuss Nozick's response to Gettier will leave the class in utter confusion. Although your discussion may be insightful, its pedagogical value will be lost on students who are insufficiently informed.

Even a well-organized presentation, however, will not succeed without a third key element: clarity. One problem is speaking too quickly. Whatever your content, if you speak too rapidly you won't be understood. Indeed, the most obvious sign of a poor lecturer is rushing. When those who are inexperienced come to a podium, they hardly ever speak at a proper pace. Yet when you hear a genuine orator, the sentences come deliberately. No student will ever object to a teacher's speaking too slowly, but many will complain if the words cascade.

Another cause of obscurity is using terms the audience doesn't understand. If I remark that for a year I worked at the NEH, which has a different mission from the NEA and is not connected to the DOJ, Washington insiders will know that I'm referring to the National Endowment for the Humanities, the National Endowment for the Arts, and the Department of Justice, but others will be lost. Should they know these acronyms? Maybe, maybe not. Either way, if many are unfamiliar with them, that's reason enough not to use them without explanation.

Imagine listening to an instructor in an introductory course who says, "To paraphrase the author of the *Pastorals*, a sparse supply of cognition is a minatory entity." Few in any class are likely to understand this remark. If the problem is pointed out to the speaker, the irritated reply may be, "It's obvious I'm referring to Alexander Pope." "But who," a student might ask, "is Alexander Pope?" At this point the instructor is likely to burst out with frustration: "How can you not know?" Perhaps needless to say, this person is not cut out to be a teacher. And even if the students were told that Pope was a celebrated eighteenth-century English poet, they probably still wouldn't realize that the teacher was paraphrasing Pope's line, "A little learning is a dangerous thing," which, in fact, may itself be unknown to many. And why use the word "minatory"? Hardly anyone will be familiar with its meaning, which is derived from the Latin word minari, meaning *to threaten*. Yet inept teachers proceed in such confusing ways all the time.

Another reason for lack of clarity is omitting steps in reasoning. Suppose an instructor of first-year students who need to brush up on algebra says, "Given that $17-11 = 3x$, we know that $2x = 4$." Many students in the class won't follow the reasoning. The teacher has failed to take the time to explain how the first equation proves that $x = 2$, thus $2 \times 2 = 4$. The teacher might respond that such reasoning is obvious. Well, it may be obvious to the teacher but not to all the students, and their understanding should be the teacher's focus.

But can't you omit what seems apparent? The question brings to mind an incident, reported by a number of witnesses, involving

Harvard professor W. V. O. Quine. His textbook on symbolic logic was widely used, and although he didn't relish teaching the subject, he was occasionally asked to do so. Once in such a course, after he wrote a proof on the board, a student raised his hand and asked impatiently, "Why bother writing out that proof? It's obvious." To which Quine replied, "Young man, this entire course is obvious."

In an introductory class, everything taught may be obvious—obvious to the teacher but not to the students. The same may sometimes be true even in a graduate seminar.

A former colleague of mine at New York University, Kai Nielsen, was highly regarded as an undergraduate and graduate teacher. When asked the key to his success, he replied, "Every course I teach is an introductory course." He meant that no matter how advanced the students were supposed to be, he never proceeded without explaining every step in his reasoning so that no one would become lost. He wasn't in the classroom to flaunt his erudition; he was there to teach.

In sum, when you find an instructor who motivates the class, organizes the material, and presents it clearly, you've found a successful teacher. And whether the class is composed of high schoolers, undergraduates, or PhD candidates, the same principles of effective teaching apply.

5

Reading the Room

YOU MAY SEEK TO motivate students, organize materials, and clarify explanations, but how do you recognize whether you are succeeding? In the world of business, the successful know how to read the room. Instructors also need that ability. They need to be aware how the class is reacting. Is the argument moving too rapidly? Has a particular example piqued their interest? Are they lost? The answers to such questions are crucial to a teacher's success.

How can you enhance your ability to read the room? Here are a few suggestions.

1. Look at your audience, not primarily at the chalkboard, the floor, the window, or the ceiling. Only by keeping your eyes on the students can you recognize their responses.
2. Use notes if necessary, but don't bury your head in them. Consult them occasionally if you prefer, but don't read them at length, thereby losing the ability to assess the audience.
3. Be aware of the reactions of all the students rather than concentrating on a select few. Try to engage everyone, not just those who regularly volunteer. A few students may display interest, but how about those who don't? Their lack of involvement is a significant feature of the situation.

4. Don't ask a question without providing the opportunity for replies. If the first answer is unsatisfactory, encourage other students to react rather than immediately answering the question yourself. After all, if no one knows the answer, perhaps the question was put ineffectively, or the students are not grasping all you had supposed.

5. Listen carefully to each student's answer. A mistake can be revelatory, suggesting a misunderstanding that may direct your further attempts at clarification. When a few students complain they are confused, the same will be true of others.

One final suggestion. In case students are not coming to your office, explain in class that to stop by for a chat they needn't have a problem. If this invitation is issued on several occasions, so as not to seem begrudging, students will appear, and teachers can then ask such questions as "How's the course going for you?" "How do you find the readings?" "Are you following the lectures?"

Listen carefully to the feedback, and don't argue but learn. After all, you may demonstrate scholarly knowledge by refuting opposing views, but you indicate pedagogical ability by skillfully reading the room.

6

Papers

In virtually every course, students are expected to complete specific assignments. An instructor should take whatever time is necessary to explain these in detail, making clear exactly what is expected. After all, if students do not do what they are supposed to, the fault is not necessarily theirs.

"Write a paper on some aspect of the course" is an irresponsible, vague direction, suggesting the professor has been either too lazy to bother thinking about suitable topics or too callous to care whether students become lost.

Should the paper be essentially a summary of other literature or a critical study of it? Does the paper depend on research in the library? If so, of what kind? How broad a topic is appropriate? How long should the paper be? Without answers to such questions, students are prone to confusion and dismay. Such problems are magnified for students who may never have written a philosophy paper. Assuming they know how is unrealistic.

To avoid chaos, distribute instructions such as these:

> In Book X of Plato's *Republic*, he refers to "an ancient quarrel" between poetry and philosophy. Drawing on the dialogues we have studied, explain Plato's reasons for supposing such a quarrel exists. If you agree with Plato's views, explain why and indicate what you believe are the

> most promising possibilities for resolving the quarrel. If you do not agree, explain your replies to the strongest counterarguments Plato or others might offer. The paper should be approximately 1,500 words and is due March 6.

This assignment is demanding but not bewildering, and students who undertake it will be able to spend their time analyzing Plato's ideas, not guessing the intentions of their instructor.

Offering students a choice of topics is fine, but offering no guidance for their project, presuming they will figure it out for themselves, is unrealistic and apt to end badly. One of the hardest tasks for scholars is finding effective topics to pursue; asking beginning students to do likewise is expecting too much.

In writing papers, students are prone to commit certain sorts of errors. Rather than waiting to correct these mistakes once they appear, why not anticipate the problems and alert students before they begin their work?

Here are some suggestions:

1. When explaining someone's views, be fair. Providing misleading versions of the positions of others, then refuting them, is pointless.
2. When quoting, do so accurately. If words are placed in quotation marks, those words need to be exact. If changes are made, use ellipses to indicate omissions and brackets to indicate additions,
3. Certain terms are so ambiguous that their use without explanation is problematic. I would include "objective," "subjective," "natural," "absolute," "relative," "relevant," "pragmatic," and "existential."
4. Anticipate possible objections to your position, then reply to them. The stronger the objections you consider and answer, the better your paper.
5. Simply quoting an authority rarely provides a satisfactory response to a criticism of your position. An explanation in your own words is usually needed.

6. Proofread your paper to avoid misspellings and typographical errors.
7. Writing with clarity is a virtue. Try to avoid wordiness and confusion.[1]

Each instructor can add to this list, but the idea is to anticipate mistakes, not wait for them to occur and then criticize.

Papers should always be returned with detailed comments. For a student to prepare material carefully, then have it given back with only a brief note such as "C: good try" is disheartening. Students are entitled to be informed which aspects of their work are well done and which unsatisfactory, as well as how future efforts might be enhanced.

Providing the chance for such improvement is reason to assign several short papers rather than a single long one. Apart from the difficulty of writing an extended piece of philosophical work, shorter papers provide students with the opportunity to learn from reactions to earlier efforts and perform better on later ones.

A related concern is the need for quick turnaround. Otherwise, students will be unable to utilize the instructor's feedback for future assignments and may even stop caring about the whole matter. Sometimes, papers sit unread, forgotten by the time the instructor gets around to grading them. This practice displays professorial negligence and promotes student alienation.

One final note. These days AI enables students to submit papers they haven't written. In the past, help could be obtained from various outside sources, such as Google, paper mills, or friends, but today the problem is more widespread. Yet the appropriate response is similar. If the class isn't too large, you can ask students to visit your office for a discussion of their paper that is apt to reveal its authorship. If, however, that procedure is not feasible, then weigh in-class examinations more heavily. We turn next to consider those.

1. Students who seek to improve their style can be advised to consult an appropriate handbook, for example, Steven M. Cahn and Victor L. Cahn, *Polishing Your Prose: How to Turn First Drafts into Finished Work* (New York: Columbia University Press, 2013).

7

Examinations

THE PURPOSE OF AN examination is to evaluate the scope and depth of a student's knowledge. Just as athletes are tested under game conditions and musicians under concert conditions, so students are tested under examination conditions to reveal whether they are in control of essential material or possess only a tenuous grasp of it. To speak glibly about a subject is not nearly as indicative of one's knowledge as to reply without prompting to pertinent questions and commit those answers to paper so they can be scrutinized.

Admittedly, exams don't challenge students in the same way as papers do, but then papers don't challenge students as exams do. Writing papers calls for the ability to present a sustained piece of philosophical thinking, a task that demands more time than is usually available for an exam. Yet rarely do papers require mastery of most or even much of the course material. Moreover, as mentioned before, students writing papers can receive help outside the classroom from sources unavailable within. For those reasons, almost all students, given the choice, opt for writing a paper rather than taking an exam. That option, however, is not always appropriate.

Granted, examinations are not the best test of imaginative power, but to suppose that original thinking flows from those uninformed about relevant fundamentals is unrealistic. Mastery of a field requires control of basic information and skills. These are the focus of effective exams.

Constructing them, though, requires care. To begin with, they should be representative of the course material. If a basic course in ethics covers Aristotle, Kant, and Mill, then the final examination should require knowledge of all three, not only the one the student prefers. Further, the questions should not be repetitive so that not knowing one answer interferes with replying to several others. The questions should also avoid ambiguity, which is why sharing the exam with a colleague ahead of time can prove useful.

Whether students should be asked to write essays or reply to a series of shorter questions is a matter of preference. If longer answers are requested, then avoid a formless query such as "Does anything in the work of Descartes help us understand ourselves?" Instead, try a sharply focused, significant question such as "Both Descartes and Berkeley raise doubts about the existence of the material world. Compare and contrast the arguments they use to raise these doubts and their conclusions as to whether their doubts can be resolved." Answering such a question requires mastery of the subject, not merely the memorization of trifles or the improvisation of hazy, high-flown vacuities.

My own preference, however, is an exam that consists of a series of short, pointed questions requiring no more than a paragraph to answer and calling for responses that are demonstrably right or wrong. Here, for example, are three items out of a dozen I presented on a test in an introductory course:

1. "If what you say is false, then anything implied by what you say is also false." Is that claim correct? If so, why? If not, why not?
2. In what way does hard determinism differ from soft determinism?
3. Does James Rachels agree that all actions are motivated by self-interest? Why?

These questions are intended to demonstrate whether students have a firm grasp of essentials or don't understand key points.

A distinct advantage of such a test is that it can be graded quickly, assigning each reply a 1 for a correct answer, 1/2 for a partially correct answer, or 0 for an incorrect answer, then summing the numbers and assigning a letter grade based on a reasonable scale. The teacher can also easily review the test in class, indicating to students the correct answers as well as the pages where they can be found. Little room remains for debate, and students can see clearly whether they are learning effectively.

While structuring an examination in this way works especially well in courses with large enrollments, I have even used the system in a graduate course in the history of political philosophy, an educational level where examinations are rarely employed. Yet I adopted this approach because I wanted students to read assiduously, mastering the details of central texts by Plato, Aristotle, Hobbes, Locke, Rousseau, Hume, Madison, Marx, Mill, Rawls, and Nozick, as well as The Declaration of Independence and the Constitution of the United States. Had I simply asked students to write a term paper, they would have been likely to concentrate on a single topic, such as Rousseau's idea of the general will or Locke's theory of property, while not bothering to do much of the rest of the reading. They wouldn't even realize how little they might have learned about the subject.

Instead, I constructed a ten-question midterm for students to assess their progress—graded but not counted unless students did well—and then a cumulative final examination with twenty-five questions along these lines:

1. "The individual is prior in the order of nature to the city." Does Aristotle agree? Why?
2. According to Hobbes, do the laws of nature oblige in foro externo? Why?
3. According to Rousseau, can a person be forced to be free? Why?

I even added a short section of quotations to be identified by author, such as the following:

> (1) "Man is born free, and everywhere he is in chains."
>
> (2) "Prudence, indeed, will dictate that governments long established should not be changed for light and transient causes; and accordingly all experience has shown that mankind are more disposed to suffer, while evils are sufferable, than to right themselves by abolishing the forms to which they are accustomed."

Some students assumed the former statement was written by Marx, but those with a firmer grasp of the material recognized it as found near the beginning of Rousseau's *Of the Social Contract*. Many assumed the longer statement to be authored by Locke, but it comes from the second paragraph of The Declaration of Independence. Weak students missed almost every quotation, stronger ones identified most, and only the most knowledgeable recognized all the passages.

While such a test of knowledge might appear to be focused excessively on details, it encouraged students to read with care, listen attentively in class as I reviewed key points of each author, and even (to my surprise) voluntarily form study groups to prepare for the exams, quizzing one another to gain mastery of these crucial works. Later, they reported how much they had learned and how pleased they were to have such a firm grasp of the fundamental texts of political philosophy.

I should, note, however, that to serve their appropriate purpose, exams at any level should not be too long. Students working at a normal pace should have time to read the questions carefully, think about them, write legible answers, and reread them. Otherwise, the examination turns into a race and loses its value. Most students should be able to hand in their papers slightly ahead of the announced finish.

Another pitfall is the omission of clear directions. Imagine sitting down to begin work and reading the following instructions: "Answer three questions from Part I and two questions from Part

II, but do not answer questions 2, 3, or 5 unless you also answer questions 8 and 9." By the time students have fully understood these directions and decided which questions to answer, they will already be short of time. Students are understandably tense and liable to misread the directions, answer the wrong questions, and bungle the proceedings. An examination should be a test of knowledge and skills, not the ability to solve verbal puzzles.

An additional problem is neglecting to announce the relative importance of each answer in grading the examination. Suppose students are required to undertake three questions but are not told that the instructor considers the third more important than the other two combined. Students may spend equal time on each, never realizing they should concentrate effort on the third. Their mistake would indicate no lack of knowledge about the subject but would result from the secret scoring system. Fairness implies that students know how much each question is worth, so they can plan their work accordingly.

One helpful grading technique is evaluating each answer booklet without knowing its author. An answer from a regularly good student may seem more impressive than the same answer from a usually poor one. Also advisable is not grading by reading from start to finish but instead judging all answers to one question at a time. Teachers will thus pay close attention to each answer rather than skimming after perusing only one or two responses. Furthermore, a teacher is less likely to alter standards for various answers to the same question than for entire tests.

As with papers, exams should be graded with comments and returned promptly, ideally at the next class meeting. Students eagerly await the outcome and, especially if they have not done well, need to become aware as soon as possible of their problems. Faculty members who procrastinate, whether from laziness or indifference, and return exams after many weeks are letting down their students.

In some philosophy courses, examinations might be out of place, whereas in others, such as elementary logic, they are the most appropriate means of assessment. In short, they are only one tool of evaluation, but their usefulness should not be overlooked.

8

Grades

MANY TEACHERS ARE UNCOMFORTABLE with grades, viewing them as inherently inaccurate devices that, in attempting to measure people, only traumatize and dehumanize them. This concern, however, is a tangle of misconceptions.

A grade represents an expert's judgment of the quality of work in a specific course. As such, it can serve not only to determine whether students are making satisfactory progress or earning academic honors but also to aid students in judging their past efforts and formulating their future plans.

Would these functions be better served if, as some have suggested, grades were replaced by written statements? In addition to the impracticality of a professor's writing hundreds of individual comments and evaluators reading thousands, the value of such reports would be severely limited if they didn't include specific indications of students' level of performance—in other words, grades. Otherwise, the notes would be more likely to reveal the teachers' literary styles than the students' academic accomplishments. Remarks one instructor considers high praise may be used indiscriminately by another, whereas comments intended as mild commendation might be mistaken as tempered criticism.

While a piece of work would not necessarily be graded identically by all specialists, members of the same department usually agree whether a student's performance has been outstanding, good, fair, poor, or unsatisfactory, the levels of achievement typically symbolized by A through F. Granted, experts sometimes disagree, but in doing so, they do not obliterate the distinction between their knowledgeable judgments and a novice's uninformed impressions.

What of the oft-repeated charge that grades are impersonal devices that reduce people to letters of the alphabet? That criticism is misguided. A grade is not a measure of a person but a person's level of achievement in a particular course. A student who receives a grade of C in introductory philosophy is not a C person with a C personality or C moral character but one whose performance in introductory philosophy was acceptable but in no way distinguished. Perhaps the student will do much better in later courses and may even excel in the study of philosophy; nevertheless, this first try was not highly successful.

Whether grades are fair, however, depends on a teacher's conscientiousness in assigning them. One potential misuse is to award grades on bases other than a student's level of achievement. Irrelevant criteria include a student's gender, race, nationality, physical appearance, dress, personality, attitudes, innate capacities, and previous academic record. None of these factors should even be considered in deciding a student's grade. Performance in the course should be the only criterion.

If an A in ancient philosophy might mean that the student tried hard, came from an impoverished community, or displayed an ingratiating personality, then the A is hopelessly ambiguous and serves no purpose. If, on the other hand, the grade signifies that the student has a firm grasp of the essentials of ancient philosophy, then the message is clear.

The most effective means for ensuring that no extraneous factors enter grading is for the instructor to make clear at the beginning of the term how final grades will be determined. How much will the final examination count? How about the papers and other short assignments? Will the student's participation be a factor? Answering these questions at the outset enables students to concentrate their energies on the most important aspects of the course, not waste time speculating about the instructor's intentions.

Yet if the announced system is unnecessarily convoluted, it can distort the purpose of the course. Suppose a teacher announces that to receive an A you need to accumulate 935 points out of 1000, and the final exam is worth 350, each of the other two exams is worth 120, each of the two papers is worth 140, and class discussion is worth 130. This proposal has the appearance of a complicated game show. Instead, this should be the rule of thumb: Explain your policy but keep matters simple.

The most common misuse of the grades is the practice commonly referred to as grading on a curve. The essence of this scheme is for the instructor to decide before the course begins what percentage of students will receive each grade. This method will produce aesthetically pleasing designs on a graph but is nevertheless conceptually confused. While a student's achievement should be judged in the light of reasonable expectations, these do not depend on such haphazard circumstances as the mix of students that happens to be taking the course concurrently.

Consider the plight of a student who earns an 80 on an exam but receives a D because most classmates scored higher. Yet the following semester in the same course, another earns an 80 with the same answers and receives an A because this time almost all classmates scored lower. Two students, identical work, different grades: the system is patently unfair.

Years ago, I overheard a student complain to his instructor about receiving a B. This nationally known scholar responded sympathetically but explained with regret that all the A's were taken. His scholarly skills exceeded his pedagogical wisdom.

Why do many instructors resort to this approach? By so doing, they avoid responsibility for determining the level of work each grade represents. They are also free to construct examinations without concern for skewed results because even if the highest grade is 30 out of 100, grading on a curve will yield apparently acceptable consequences. Yet the appearance is deceiving because rank in class will have been confused with mastery of subject. The procrustean practice of grading on a curve rests on this muddle and should be abandoned (although inept teaching or badly constructed examinations should not result in unconscionably low grades).

A different distortion of the grading system, rare nowadays, is an unwillingness to award high grades. Instructors who adopt this attitude take pride in rigor. But just as a high school student who receives an A in mathematics need not be the equal of Isaac Newton, so a first-year college student may receive an A in writing without being the equal of George Orwell. Receiving an A only means that, judged by reasonable standards, the student has done excellent work. An instructor who rarely rewards high grades is failing to distinguish good from poor performance. This proclivity does not uphold academic standards but only misinterprets the grading symbols, thereby undermining their appropriate functions.

A more common misuse of grades is the reluctance to award low grades, a practice popularly known as grade inflation. It results from the unwillingness of instructors to give students the bad news that they have not done as well as they might have hoped. Yet maintaining academic standards rests on the willingness of professors to tell the truth. Understandably, some are concerned about the possible injustice of giving their own students realistic grades while other students receive inflated ones. The solution, adopted at some colleges, is for transcripts to include not only a student's course grade but also the average grade for all students in that section of the course. This way exposes grade inflation and dissipates unfairness. In any case, each instructor who inflates grades adds to the problem.

Yet awarding grades also calls for a sense of fair play. Consider a professor I knew who gave relatively easy exams throughout the semester, thereby leading students to believe they were doing well. The final exam, however, was vastly more difficult, and many students were shocked and angered to receive low grades for the course. Clearly, this instructor misled and harmed his students. He was akin to a storeowner who announces a major sale but applies low prices to only a few rarely sought items.

After all, ethics applies not only to physicians, nurses, lawyers, business managers, journalists, and engineers but also to teachers. They, too, can lie, mislead, and fail to fulfill all manner of professional responsibilities. Indeed, classrooms are no more free of misconduct than hospitals, courts, or boardrooms.

Grading is especially sensitive to mishandling because assessments are done privately and results are not easily challenged. Teachers, therefore, need to make every effort to treat students equitably.

9

A Teacher's Role

THE AIM OF TEACHING is education, not indoctrination. For a teacher to defend personal beliefs is appropriate, but regarding any disputed issue, students should be provided with the strongest reasons behind opposing positions, then encouraged to develop their own views. Forcing anyone to accept the teacher's opinion regarding a debated matter is professorial malpractice.

For instance, the teacher may be a materialist, but students should be made aware of the arguments for dualism; the teacher may be a liberal, but students should be made aware of the arguments for a conservative position; the teacher may support abortion rights, but students should be made aware of the arguments for a right to life. Those who have not learned how to explain the reasoning of their opponents on controversial matters have not been well-taught.

This principle was exemplified for me on one occasion when I taught a graduate seminar in philosophy of religion. The class included a gentleman from India who frequently contributed insights about Hinduism. I assumed he was a Hindu and welcomed his perceptive comments regarding that religious tradition. After all the classes ended, he came to my office and expressed his appreciation for the course. When I thanked him for enriching our discussion by providing the perspective of a Hindu, he explained that he was not a Hindu; rather, he was a Catholic priest from a Christian community in southern India. He explained that he had not revealed his religious identity because he did not want to inhibit anyone from expressing skepticism about Christianity.

I was surprised, but he told me that while he knew I was not Christian, he believed I had done justice to those who were and had demonstrated that my assessment of anyone's work did not depend on whatever religious beliefs they might defend or oppose. I was gratified by this assurance.

Professors in every course should present the material in a balanced way and not penalize any students because they do not share the teacher's viewpoint. As a test, an instructor is well-advised to imagine that intellectual opponents were in the classroom. Would they recognize the instructor's version of their position? Would they agree that at least some of their arguments had been adequately explained? Would they consider the evaluations of student work justifiable? If not, the instructor should make fairness a higher priority.

On the other hand, students should not be led to suppose that all expressed opinions are equally viable. Some arguments are valid, others invalid. Some hypotheses are well-founded, others not. A claim may be self-contradictory, run counter to the available evidence, be unclear, or mean nothing at all. Fair-mindedness does not require obliterating the differences between clarity and obscurity, accuracy and carelessness, knowledge and ignorance. Instructors should be willing to insist on these distinctions.

Overlooking them due to concern about the possible effects of criticism on a student's psyche misunderstands the professor's role. Granted, some students are emotionally unstable. But in those cases, we need to remember that a philosopher is not a clinical psychologist. Students dealing with a personal difficulty should be advised to visit the school's counseling service rather than be treated by a medical tyro, however well-meaning. Philosophers do not presume to practice surgery; they should also refrain from psychiatry.

One issue about the proper relationship between teacher and student demands special attention, having been the source of some of the most egregious instances of professorial malfeasance. I refer to the view that teachers ought to be friends with their students. The problem with this approach, Sidney Hook pointed out, is that teachers "must be friendly without becoming a friend, although [they] may pave the way for later friendship, for friendship is a mark of preference and expresses itself in indulgence, favors, and distinctions that unconsciously find an invidious form."[1] Faculty members ought to care about the progress of each student, but they should remain dispassionate, able to deliberate, judge, and act without thought of personal interest or advantage. Even the appearance of partiality is likely to impair the learning process by damaging an instructor's credibility, causing students to doubt that standards are being applied fairly.

Thus, every teacher should be scrupulous in ensuring that no student receives preferential treatment. If one student is permitted to write a paper instead of taking an exam, that option should be available to everyone in the class. If one is allowed to turn in an assignment late, then all others in similar circumstances should be offered the same opportunity. And if one student is invited to the professor's home for dinner, then everyone should receive similar invitations. Adherence to this rule never leads to trouble; breaking it is frequently problematic.

One obvious implication of the principle of equal consideration is that between teacher and student not only is friendship inappropriate but even more so is romance. Even if a student from the same college never enrolls in a professor's classes, their liaison suggests that this faculty member does not view students from a professional standpoint. If an attempt is made to keep the relationship secret, the professor's integrity is compromised. In any case, such efforts at concealment almost always fail, thus besmirching the professor's reputation for honesty.

1. Sidney Hook, *Education for Modern Man: A New Perspective* (1963; Eugene, OR: Wipf and Stock, 2020), 230–231.

If a student seeks to initiate an affair with a professor, the only proper response is an unequivocal refusal. On the other hand, for a professor to attempt to seduce or coerce a student into having an affair is an egregious abuse of authority that provides strong grounds for dismissal.

When a student leaves the college or moves to a different unit of the university, whatever personal contact may develop with a professor is up to the two of them. During the years of undergraduate or graduate study, however, the only appropriate relationship is professional. To maintain these boundaries is in everyone's best interest.

For whatever reasons, philosophers have recently had more than their share of scandals involving forms of sexual harassment or abuse. Under these unfortunate circumstances, those who teach philosophy should be especially vigilant to maintain their proper function as guides through a field of study. They should not seek or accept the role of psychiatrist, friend, or lover.

10

Teaching Graduate Students

While my emphasis in this work is primarily on teaching undergraduates (a subject I'll return to shortly), we should not overlook issues that arise in graduate education. There the quality of instruction is frequently disappointing.

The source of the problem is that professors too often presume that teaching at an advanced level transcends the need to observe principles of good pedagogy. Thus, motivation may be omitted as unnecessary, organization denigrated as prosaic, and clarification spurned as simplistic. No wonder graduate students find many of their classes dreary, bewildering, or disheartening.

Indeed, too many graduate teachers seek ways to discharge their pedagogical duties with minimal effort. One method defended as increasing participation is delegating to a different student each week the responsibility for summarizing the given readings and leading the conversation. Others in the class are likely not to bother, then, reading closely in advance of the seminar or listening attentively there to a peer's halting attempt to guide the discussion.

Another strategy for the reluctant professor is to find a faculty member willing to offer a team-taught course. The work is shared, and the class is supposed to benefit from listening to a conversation between colleagues. The exchange, however, is likely to assume background knowledge shared by the faculty but unfamiliar to the students.

If even this device is too demanding, a professor can invite other scholars from inside or outside the school to give lectures. Such a colloquium can be framed as offering students the opportunity to hear differing points of view, but such talks are too often idiosyncratic rather than pedagogically useful. Meanwhile, the professor assigned to teach the class receives credit for having done so.

If such a joint approach is not feasible, professors can still avoid teaching by considering any graduate course, even a first-level one, primarily as an opportunity for developing their own research and enlisting supporters in the effort to work on its fine points. For instance, an instructor may decide to distribute chapters of the instructor's own forthcoming book and ask students to help edit the manuscript. Such an approach may provide students with insights into recent scholarship, but the question that doesn't even arise is whether this procedure is the best way to promote a thorough and balanced understanding of a field's fundamental methods and materials. As a result, graduate students may also be led to suppose that their professor's opinions dominate the field, only to find later perhaps that competing views are at least as influential.

This egocentric style of graduate instruction is also flawed in suggesting to students that professional success depends on sharing their instructors' intellectual outlooks. Professors should not attempt to attract devoted bands of personal disciples; that goal is appropriate for gurus. Graduate faculty members should hope to foster a future generation of well-informed, independent-minded scholars, and courses should be conducted to achieve that aim.

A most unfortunate side effect of much graduate teaching is conveying to students the message that ignorance is ignominious. If students admit that they are unfamiliar with a particular author, work, concept, or position, then they risk ridicule. Thus, to maintain their dignity, even when confused, they are encouraged to feign understanding by nodding knowingly instead of confessing,

"I'm unfamiliar with that philosopher," "I don't know the book you cited," "I'm not following the argument you presented." In short, contra Socrates, the goal is always to appear knowledgeable.

The opposite, however, ought to be the case. Professors should encourage students to indicate in class whenever they are lost. Such admissions should be met not with a put-down but with a compliment for intellectual honesty. After all, those afraid to admit what they do not know are defenseless against others who indulge in obfuscation.

These days, signs around the country tell us that if we see something, we should say something. Graduate students should be urged to follow an analogous rule: If you don't understand something, say something.

The most critical area of a graduate professor's responsibility is advising students on their doctoral dissertations, and here horror stories are legion. These include the typical tale of the advisor who suggests a topic so difficult that it would take decades to complete, or does not return a student's work for many months, or insists that drafts be endlessly revised without making clear the problems. Students subjected to such treatment can become so frustrated, resentful, and angry that they find continuing their work impossible.

Advisors should help, not hinder, progress. While not approving poor work, they should encourage students to improve it expeditiously. Granted, advising outstanding students is a delight, but not all students will excel. Yet, with assistance most can complete the task at hand in an acceptable manner. The aim is to help them do so, not make their lives miserable with criticism for failing to attain levels of achievement beyond their reach.

A common problem is lack of a suitable topic. Typically, students want to tackle one of vast magnitude, thereby making completion a virtual impossibility. The effective advisor is aware of this tendency and offers students alternatives that are far easier to manage. After all, when a PhD is awarded, the diploma doesn't indicate the scope of the dissertation or how long a student labored to complete it. The idea is to finish and move on to a career.

My experience has been that the undertaking should take twelve to eighteen months; beyond two years is excessive. An effective advisor encourages students to finish in that time frame and enables them to do so. Drafts should be returned promptly, criticisms should be constructive rather than destructive, and the process should be demanding, not demoralizing. Indeed, in some cases, a student may find that working with a supportive advisor to complete a dissertation is a highlight of doctoral education.

Dissertation supervisors are expected to write letters for their advisees as they seek an academic position. But what if a student's work has been no more than satisfactory? In that case, a candid letter might doom all prospects.

In such circumstances, George Sher offers this advice: "To do what we can for our weaker students, we can try to write letters that will not disqualify them outright and that may be overlooked if their other letters come in stronger, while to preserve at least a tenuous connection to the truth, we can avoid saying things that are flatly false while playing up every scrap of positive information that is even marginally relevant."[1]

His advice accurately captures common practice, but is it justifiable? I believe so, but to avoid misunderstanding we need to distinguish two types of evaluations: assessments and recommendations. An assessment is written about someone with whom you have no personal relationship (or none that influences you) and is expected to be a forthright judgment of the individual's merits. If, for example, you are asked whether someone is qualified to be granted tenure, you should provide a full account of the individual's strengths and weaknesses as you see them. If, in your view, the individual does not merit tenure, you should say so without fudging.

A letter of recommendation, however, is understood by all to be written in support of a candidate. You are expected to make the best case you can while avoiding misrepresentation. After all,

1. George Sher, "Global Norming: An Inconvenient Truth," in Robert B. Talisse and Maureen Eckert, eds., *A Teacher's Life: Essays for Steven M. Cahn* (2009; Eugene, OR: Wipf and Stock Publishers, 2021), 110.

if you are identified as the candidate's advisor or supportive dissertation committee member, you are expected to defend your approval by painting a positive picture rather than dwelling on an individual's weaknesses.

In brief, when asked to provide an evaluation, be sure to understand whether you are being asked for an assessment or a recommendation. Failure to recognize this distinction results in the sort of remark I once saw in a letter of recommendation for a faculty position: "Arthur [a pseudonym] is not among the best students I have taught, but he is not among the worst either." Although the faculty member actually thought rather well of Arthur and had been more than willing to write in his behalf, that remark doomed Arthur's chances. The writer had confused a recommendation with an assessment, thereby stating what was true yet inappropriate.

II

Teaching Introductory Philosophy

SHIFTING OUR ATTENTION FROM graduate students to beginners, we turn to the issue of deciding what material to cover in teaching introductory philosophy. Here are some options.

When I taught at Vassar College in the mid-1960s, every student who wished to take philosophy was required to begin with a two-semester sequence in the history of philosophy. The first semester concentrated on Plato and Aristotle, as well as their immediate predecessors and successors, while the second semester focused on Descartes, Spinoza, Leibniz, Locke, Berkeley, Hume, and Kant. Virtually every member of the department taught this demanding course. Although to be fully prepared, most instructors had to put in extra work, all students obtained a strong foundation. Furthermore, teachers in every subsequent philosophy course could rely on all their students possessing a thorough knowledge of the history of philosophy.

Structured in this way, introductory philosophy provides historical perspective, and students are apt to be excited by the array of great books and ideas. Ancient and modern philosophy are given their due, and students read in chronological order many works that have strongly influenced the development of Western thought.

Not surprisingly, students are more easily motivated to read a classic text by a renowned thinker rather than an article by a recent scholar unknown to them. Further, most great works of the past, unlike contemporary journal articles, were not intended only for specialists. They embody a breadth of vision that has inspired generations, and reading at least some of these works in their entirety is intellectually fulfilling.

This approach, however, also has its disadvantages. It suggests that philosophy is mainly the contemplation of works written long ago, and students may be led to suppose that their sole obligation is to grasp what others have said, not to think critically. This problem is magnified by the need to spend much time and effort struggling with unfamiliar terminology and seeking to understand the concerns that motivated our intellectual forebears. Philosophy can thus be turned into a tour of the past rather than an active inquiry of present importance.

I have known highly educated persons who in school studied great works of philosophy and admired the subject. Yet they are unfamiliar with either the concerns or methods of contemporary philosophy. An introductory course is not entirely satisfying if it leaves these matters as unexplored territory.

A second approach is embodied in the following proposal: "To me, Socrates and Plato are the greatest philosophers in the history of Western philosophy. If I am right, there could be no better introduction to philosophy than studying their theories."[1] The author then recommends an introductory course in which students are asked to read eleven dialogues of Plato: *Symposium, Phaedrus, Lysis, Euthyphro, Apology, Theaetetus, Republic, Charmides, Protagoras, Phaedo,* and *Crito.*

Let's assume the truth of the premise. Does the conclusion follow? Compare this analogous argument:

> To me, J. S. Bach is the greatest composer in the history of music. If I am right, there could be no better introduction to music than studying his compositions. Hence, I recommend that a first course in music focus on the following works by Bach: a cantata, an orchestral suite, a Brandenburg Concerto, a toccata and fugue for organ, a

1. Sahar Joakim, "Introduction to Philosophy," APA Blog (May 29, 2019).

> suite for solo cello, a partita for solo violin, the Concerto for Two Violins, and selections from the Goldberg Variations, the St. Matthew Passion, the Mass in B Minor, and the Art of Fugue.

The problem in both cases is that the eminence of a particular figure does not imply the pedagogical appropriateness of offering beginners only one main avenue to understanding the subject.

The case for such a concentrated approach reminds me of a session many years ago at the Eastern Division Meeting of the American Philosophical Association where Fred Feldman explained his practice of requiring students in an introductory course to read and critique only one book: Descartes' *Meditations on First Philosophy.* No doubt Professor Feldman thought highly of the work, yet the problem with making it the sole reading was unintentionally revealed by his commentator, Alasdair MacIntyre. He first praised Feldman's strategy of focusing on a single masterpiece but expressed dismay that Feldman had picked the wrong one: He had selected the *Meditations* rather than MacIntyre's choice: Plato's *Republic.*

The problem is that, had MacIntyre been a student in Feldman's course, he would have been unhappy spending the entire semester discussing a single book that he didn't find especially illuminating, while Feldman would have had the same reaction had he been a student in MacIntyre's course. In any case, even a good thing overdone can become boring, and beginners may find excruciating an entire course devoted exclusively to one book or author.

Not all students find the same material appealing; therefore, they are more likely to appreciate an array of perspectives on the subject. An advanced seminar might appropriately focus on a single text or author, but an introductory course is intended to arouse the interest of as many participants as possible, and a narrow set of readings is unlikely to achieve that goal.

Granted, courses can cover only limited ground, but varied content is a pedagogical virtue. Although a particular philosophy professor may be more interested in free will rather than personal identity or the problem of induction, assuming the goal is to engage students in philosophical inquiry, why not cover all three topics and perhaps spark interest in at least one? Few are inspired by every philosophical author or subject, and unfortunate, indeed, is a student who might potentially have been excited by philosophy but is not offered the opportunity to study more than the part of the field with which the instructor happens to be most comfortable.

Beginning students need to be motivated, and no one topic or author will work best for all. By offering more possibilities, chances are greater that at least some aspect of the reading will prove stimulating. Therefore, in planning an introductory course, if you are uncertain whether to cover more topics or study fewer subjects in greater depth, remember that for most beginners, variety enhances vitality.

A third format uses a single-authored textbook written with a student audience in mind. The advantage of this approach is that reading a contemporary synopsis of philosophical problems is far easier to understand than the original works.

The problem, though, is that, unlike calculus or accounting, philosophy does not offer a body of accepted truths, and one author can hardly do justice to all competing viewpoints. Admittedly, philosophy can be difficult to understand, and a textbook can ease the strain. On the other hand, philosophical disagreement is best grasped by confronting various authors who have different styles and opinions. Furthermore, a homogenized textbook designed to avoid taking controversial stands is apt to lead students to wonder why the author appears indecisive.

A key feature of the study of philosophy is that good reasons can be given for opposing positions. Students need to recognize this feature of the subject. When they ask, "Who's right?" they should be led to understand that just as each member of a trial jury needs to decide upon and defend a view after considering all the relevant evidence, so each philosophical inquirer needs to decide upon and defend a view after considering all the relevant arguments.

John Stuart Mill observed that we should hear opposing views "from persons who actually believe them, who defend them in earnest, and do their very utmost for them."[2] Because bringing proponents of clashing views to the classroom is usually not feasible, teachers can at least provide readings in which opposing opinions are presented as plausibly as possible. Achieving this goal when all views are expressed in one voice is a challenge.

The most popular approach to teaching introductory philosophy is to use an anthology in which readings are grouped by topic and drawn from historical and contemporary sources. Students thereby become acquainted with major problems of philosophy, read important historical and contemporary writing on each subject, and are encouraged to think through issues for themselves. Historical philosophers are given a word but not the last word; contemporary philosophers are seen as innovators but not creators ex nihilo.

This approach, however, has its pitfalls. As students shift quickly from Aristotle to Locke to Nozick, they are tempted to treat these authors as contemporaries. Students can also lose hold of the threads that are supposed to connect the selections. Furthermore, excerpts taken out of context can be difficult to understand. Importantly, the approach may do a disservice to major historical figures because reading a few pages from a philosophical classic is somewhat akin to listening to a few pages from a great symphony—the overall effect is typically disappointing.

Despite these problems, books of readings remain a popular choice for teaching introductory philosophy because they afford instructors the opportunity to cover many topics and authors, thus displaying the range of philosophical inquiry. Still, graduate students, who are often unfamiliar with the available anthologies, need to be reminded that books vary enormously in difficulty.

Over the years, I have joined with various colleagues to edit four such collections, but a volume widely used today is my own *Exploring Philosophy*.[3] In what follows, I use that book as background to discuss topics usually covered in introductory courses.

2. John Stuart Mill, *On Liberty* (Lanham, MD: Rownan & Littlefield, 2005), 64.

3. *Exploring Philosophy*, Eighth Edition, ed. Steven M. Cahn (New York: Oxford University Press, 2024).

12

Teaching Reasoning

As most students taking their first philosophy course usually have no idea or, worse, a mistaken idea, of the nature of the subject, the first readings provide an orientation. I like the essay by Monroe and Elizabeth Lane Beardsley[1] because it is remarkably clear and will leave no one behind. Other instructors may prefer starting with Russell's inspirational chapter from *The Problems of Philosophy*[2] or Plato's *Defence of Socrates*,[3] which has the advantage of historical and philosophical importance but requires background information that some may not wish to take time to provide.

Then comes an important decision: Which area of philosophy to approach first? One choice is epistemology, although I myself find it difficult to motivate students to consider whether the table we sense is the real table. Others may prefer a metaphysical issue, such as the nature of the human mind, but I fear that the complexities of that subject, even in the capable hands of Paul M. Churchland,[4] may prove overwhelming.

1. "What Is Philosophy?" in Cahn, 3–8.
2. "The Value of Philosophy," in Cahn, 8–11.
3. *Defence of Socrates,* in Cahn, 112–137.
4. "The Mind-Body Problem," in Cahn, 174–186.

My preference, instead, is to begin with the elements of reasoning. Every philosophical issue involves argument, and I want to ensure that all students are familiar with the concepts of premise, conclusion, validity, and soundness so that these terms can be used consistently throughout the course.

The key idea, which requires emphasis because it is counterintuitive, is that a valid argument can contain false premises and a true conclusion. To try to ensure that students grasp this point, after explaining it as clearly as I can, I move quickly around the room challenging students:

1. Give me an invalid argument with two true premises and a true conclusion.
2. Give me a valid argument with two false premises and a false conclusion.
3. Give me a valid argument with two false premises and a true conclusion.
4. Give me a valid argument with one false premise and a true conclusion.
5. Give me a valid argument with one true premise, one false premise, and a false conclusion.
6. Give me a valid argument with one true premise, one false premise, and a true conclusion.
7. Give me a valid argument with a true premise and a false conclusion. (You can't. Why?)

Soon most students understand the nature of a valid argument and realize the possibility of its having false premises and a true conclusion. The exercise is accessible and possibly enjoyable or even humorous.

Next, I turn to a fallacy many logic books bypass but is committed all too frequently. I refer to the confusion of necessary and sufficient conditions. How often, for instance, do you hear someone remark that the government need not increase money for a particular purpose, perhaps national defense or the fight against poverty, because even with additional funds success may not be achieved? In other words, more money isn't necessary because it isn't sufficient.

When I sought a brief article on this subject to include in *Exploring Philosophy*, I found none, so I wrote my own that reflects the presentation I would make in class. Of course, I wouldn't deal with the issue by simply saying to the students, "I'm sure you all can see that even if A is a necessary condition for B, A may not be a sufficient condition for B. So let's move on to more interesting material." I wouldn't classify that approach as bad teaching; it isn't even teaching. Telling something to someone who lacks the background to understand what you are saying is just talking, not teaching.

As to motivating this topic, I remark how often even sophisticated thinkers commit this fallacy. Then I define necessary condition and sufficient condition, providing clear examples of each.

> One state of affairs, A, is a necessary condition for another state of affairs, B, if B cannot occur without A occurring. For instance, in the United States a person must be at least eighteen years old before being entitled to vote. In other words, being eighteen is a necessary condition for being entitled to vote.
>
> One state of affairs, A, is a sufficient condition for another state of affairs, B, if the occurrence of A ensures the occurrence of B. For instance, in an American presidential election, for a candidate to receive 300 electoral votes ensures that candidate's election. In other words, receiving 300 electoral votes is a sufficient condition for winning the election.

The next step is to emphasize the difference between necessary and sufficient conditions and provide further examples.

> Note that even if A is a necessary condition for B, A need not be a sufficient condition for B. For instance, even if you need to be eighteen to vote, you also need to be a citizen of the United States. Thus, being eighteen is necessary but not sufficient for voting.

> Similarly, even if A is a sufficient condition for B, A need not be a necessary condition for B. For instance, if a presidential candidate receives 300 electoral votes, then that candidate is elected, but receiving 300 electoral votes, while sufficient for election, is not necessary, because a candidate who receives 299 votes is also elected.

Next comes an example of how necessary and sufficient conditions may be muddled.

> Confusing necessary and sufficient conditions is a common mistake in reasoning. If one individual argues that extensive prior experience in Washington, DC, is required for a person to be a worthy presidential candidate, that claim is not refuted by pointing out that many candidates with such experience have not been worthy. To refute the claim that experience is necessary for worthiness requires demonstrating not that many with experience have been unworthy but that a person without experience has been worthy. After all, the original claim was that experience is necessary, not sufficient.

A further insight is that if you provide necessary and sufficient conditions for a term, then it has been defined.

> Suppose A is both necessary and sufficient for B. For example, being a rectangle with all four sides equal is necessary and sufficient for being a square. In other words, a geometric figure cannot be a square unless it is a rectangle with four sides equal, and if a rectangle has all four sides equal, then it is a square. Thus, a satisfactory definition of "square" is "rectangle with all four sides equal."

The final step in teaching necessary and sufficient conditions is the hardest to grasp yet essential to understanding the relationship of the two concepts. Before presenting it, I alert students to the challenge it presents.

> Here is an additional twist. What is the difference between asserting that A is a necessary condition for B and that B is a sufficient condition for A? Nothing. These are two ways of saying that the occurrence of B ensures the

> occurrence of A. Furthermore, what is the difference between asserting that A is a sufficient condition for B and that B is a necessary condition for A? Again, nothing. These are two ways of saying that the occurrence of A ensures the occurrence of B.

For emphasis, I then remind students of the most common error so they will be less prone to commit it.

> The critical mistake is thinking that if A is necessary for B, then A is sufficient for B. Or that if A is sufficient for B, then A is necessary for B. These are fallacies, errors in reasoning.

And now, I offer one additional example that helps students grasp the overall sense of the discussion:

> The next time you hear someone say, for example, that you can be well educated without knowing any logic because some people who know logic are not well educated, you can point out that the speaker has confused necessary and sufficient conditions. Just because some people who know logic are not well educated does not prove that you can be well educated without knowing logic. That conclusion would only follow if some people who don't know logic are nevertheless well educated.

When the presentation is completed, you can test your students and your own pedagogical skill by asking the class these questions.

1. If A is a necessary condition for B, is B always a necessary condition for A?
2. If A is a necessary condition for B, is B always a sufficient condition for A?
3. Is the claim that the study of philosophy is necessary for happiness undermined by presenting cases of unhappy people who have studied philosophy?
4. Present your own example of the fallacy of confusing necessary and sufficient conditions.

If most students can answer these questions, your teaching has succeeded. If they can't, then you have failed.

I am not suggesting, of course, that this presentation is the best or only way of explaining this material. Others may have a more engaging or effective approach.

If, on the other hand, you do not find such pedagogical matters of interest, do not wish to be bothered with offering such elementary explanations, or do not care whether as many students as possible have mastered such basic material, then regardless of your philosophical skills, you are likely to be ineffective in the classroom.

13

Teaching Free Will

WHICHEVER METAPHYSICAL OR EPISTEMOLOGICAL issues you choose to discuss will be difficult for beginners. I myself have had most success with the problem of free will and determinism. It has the following pedagogical advantages: Its presentation in the form of an argument with two premises and a conclusion can be brief; its most obvious solutions can each be explained as plausible but together incompatible; its connection to issues about moral and legal responsibility can easily be made apparent. The essence of the presentation I offer to students is found in my article "Freedom or Determinism?"[1]

For motivation, I use the famous 1924 Leopold and Loeb case to tie the issue to a practical context and illustrate how philosophical issues can arise outside a classroom. Most students will respond, whether positively or negatively, to Clarence Darrow's appeal on behalf of his privileged and precocious clients, who confessed to the murder of Loeb's fourteen-year old cousin:

> I do not know what it was that made these boys do this mad act, but I do know there is a reason for it. I know they did not beget themselves. I know that any one of an infinite number of causes reaching back to the beginning

1. Cahn, 223–232.

> might be working out in these boys' minds, whom you are asked to hang in malice and in hatred and in injustice, because someone in the past has sinned against them . . . What had this boy to do with it? He was not his own father; he was not his own mother; he was not his own grandparents. All of this was handed to him. He did not surround himself with governesses and wealth. He did not make himself. And yet he is to be compelled to pay.[2]

As happened in the more than one hundred cases in which Darrow defended someone charged with murder, his clients were spared the death penalty. (On a historical note, immediately after the Leopold and Loeb case, Darrow defended John T. Scopes, charged in a Dayton, Tennessee, courtroom with the crime of teaching evolution.)

The key to Darrow's position is that if the argument he utilized is sound, then not only were Leopold and Loeb not to blame for what they had done, but no persons are ever to blame for any of their actions. That observation leads to formulating the basis of Darrow's argument as follows:

> Premise 1: No action is free if it must occur.
> Premise 2: In the case of every event that occurs, antecedent conditions, known or unknown, ensure the event's occurrence.
> Conclusion: Therefore, no action is free.

Here, the previous work on validity and soundness comes into play, and these questions can be asked: Is the argument valid? Is it sound? As students will recognize, the argument is valid because the conclusion follows from the premises, but are the premises true?

If you believe so, then you are, to use the terminology of William James, a hard determinist.[3] In other words, you accept determinism, believe determinism incompatible with free will, and conclude that human beings never act freely. If, on the other hand,

2. *Attorney for the Damned,* ed. Arthur Weinberg (New York: Simon and Schuster, 1957), 37, 65.

3. See William James, "The Dilemma of Determinism," in Cahn, 251–263.

you accept determinism but believe it compatible with free will, then you are a soft determinist. But what if you believe in free will but don't consider it compatible with determinism? Then you are a libertarian.

The upshot is that each of the three agrees partially and disagrees partially with each of the other two. The hard determinist and soft determinist agree that determinism is true but disagree as to whether it is compatible with freedom. The hard determinist and libertarian agree that the two doctrines are incompatible but disagree as to which is true. The soft determinist and libertarian agree that people have free will but disagree as to whether freedom is compatible with determinism.

One of the three would appear to be correct and the other two wrong, But whose position is most persuasive? Each has a burden to shoulder.

In particular, hard determinism must overcome the plausible claim that, for instance, while attending a lecture it is within my power to raise my hand to ask a question and also within my power not to do so. The decision is up to me, but in that case I am free to raise my hand, a refutation of hard determinism.

Soft determinism must overcome the plausible claim that if my actions are the result of a causal claim extending back before my birth, then I am not now free regarding any action. Thus, determinism and free will are incompatible.

The libertarian must overcome the plausible claim that every event is caused, whether a loud noise, a change in the weather, or a human action. If the events hadn't been caused, they wouldn't have occurred. Thus, because determinism and free will are incompatible and determinism is true, free will is false.

As the class proceeds, we consider each position in turn, discussing whether it can meet the challenge it faces. Can the hard determinist explain the widespread sense that we sometimes act freely? (The reading by Thomas Nagel[4] considers this concern). Can the soft determinist demonstrate how determinism and free

4. "Free Will," in Cahn, 215–220.

will can both be true? (The readings from Hume[5] and W. T. Stace[6] are intended to bolster that position.) Can the libertarian explain how human behavior can be understood if it is not caused? Here I appeal to a possible distinction between reasons and causes, suggesting that while causes can explain why a machine malfunctions, perhaps only reasons can explain why a human being stops work as a protest.

Thus, we end this unit, having tried to make the best possible case for each of the three alternatives and leaving the matter for each student to reach a judgment. The lesson here is that although philosophical questions are perplexing, understanding their difficulties strengthens one's ability to think critically about fundamental issues. What if some believe that their solution to a philosophical problem avoids all difficulties? In that case, I would suggest that they haven't fully understood the problem.

I don't mix my discussion of determinism with the issue of fatalism. Although my earliest full-length work was devoted to that subject,[7] my experience has been that students are likely to become bewildered as they struggle to understand such intricacies as competing interpretations of Aristotle's account of future contingencies. Nevertheless, a question may arise regarding the difference between the two doctrines, and most reference books provide an inadequate account of the matter.

For example, *The Oxford Dictionary of Philosophy*, Third Edition, edited by Simon Blackburn, contains the following entry:

> **fatalism** The doctrine that what will be will be, or that human action has no influence on events. 'Either a bullet has my number on it or it does not; if it does, then there is no point taking precautions for it will kill me anyhow; if it does not then there is no point taking precautions for it is not going to kill me; hence either way there is no point taking precautions.' The dilemma ignores the highly likely possibility that whether the bullet has your

5. "An Enquiry Concerning Human Understanding," in Cahn, 243–251.

6. "Free Will and Determinism," in Cahn, 220–222.

7. *Fate, Logic, and Time* (1967; Eugene, OR: Wipf and Stock, 2004).

> number on it depends on whether you take precautions. Fatalism is wrongly confused with determinism, which by itself carries no implications that human action is ineffectual.

The first definition offered is a tautology, "what will be will be"; if that thesis is fatalism, then the doctrine is true but uninteresting. The second definition, "human action has no influence on events," is clearly false, because, for example, obtaining a divorce logically requires getting married. Examples like that of the bullet were known in antiquity as the "idle argument," and the appropriate reply, given by the Stoic logician Chrysippus, is that taking precautions may save you, and, if so, then they were fated to do so. Hence, such examples provide no refutation of fatalism. Furthermore, the difference between fatalism and determinism is not that fatalism claims human action is ineffectual but that fatalism makes no reference to causation. Moreover, some determinists affirm free will, but all fatalists deny it.

The entry in *The Oxford Companion to Philosophy*, New Edition, edited by Ted Honderich, is no more helpful.

> **fatalism** The belief, not to be confused with causal determinism, that deliberation and action are pointless because the future will be the same no matter what we do. According to the famous "idle argument" of antiquity, 'If it is fated for you to recover from this illness, you will recover whether you call in a doctor or not; similarly, if it is fated for you not to recover from this illness, you will not recover whether you call in a doctor or not; and either your recovery or non-recovery is fated; therefore there is no point in calling in a doctor.' Thus all actions and choices are 'idle' because they cannot affect the future. Determinists reject fatalism on the grounds that it may be determined that we can be cured only by calling the doctor.

Here fatalism is identified with the "idle argument," as though that piece of reasoning is itself the fatalistic position. In fact, the "idle argument" is a supposed refutation of fatalism, easily answered with the response of Chrysippus that, for example, whether you call a doctor is as fated as whether you recover.

Fortunately, the proper understanding of fatalism can be found in the *Encyclopedia of Ethics*, Second Edition, edited by Lawrence C. Becker and Charlotte B. Becker. There, the extended entry "fate and fatalism," authored by John Martin Fischer, begins: "Fatalism can be understood as the doctrine that it is a logical or conceptual truth that agents are never free to do other than what they actually do." Note the following key points in Fischer's definition. First, fatalism is not a form of determinism. Second, fatalism denies free will on the basis of conceptual considerations. Third, fatalism does not affirm or imply that human actions have no influence on future events.

The key question, of course, is whether fatalism, appropriately understood, can be supported by a philosophically sophisticated argument. The most celebrated contemporary attempt was authored in 1962 by Richard Taylor, whose accessible article "Fatalism" in *The Philosophical Review* generated heated discussion in a host of leading journals. More than two decades later, a detailed contribution to the controversy was offered in a senior thesis at Amherst College submitted by the soon-to-be-celebrated writer David Foster Wallace. It was reprinted along with highlights of the original philosophical debate in *Fate, Time, and Language: An Essay on Free Will.*[8]

In sum, fatalism is neither a tautology nor a preposterous claim about the ineffectiveness of human action. Rather, it is a challenging thesis denying free will on the basis of conceptual considerations and requiring for its assessment a careful exploration of issues regarding time, logic, and freedom. I myself wouldn't attempt to untangle the complexities in an introductory course but would focus on determinism and leave fatalism for another occasion.

8. Eds., Steven M. Cahn and Maureen Eckert (New York: Columbia University Press, 2011).

14

Teaching Philosophy of Religion

RECOGNIZING DIFFICULTIES IN ONE'S position is especially challenging in religious matters, and therefore I prefer turning to that subject only after having explored at least one other issue where personal commitment does not run so deep. In any case, eventually, the time comes for discussing aspects of philosophy of religion. Here motivation is not a problem because the topic matters so much to so many.

The routine approach is to present and assess the three traditional arguments for the existence of God. Then the focus shifts to the problem of evil, after which the unit on God's existence ends.

This common way of proceeding often occurs within a set of misleading assumptions that may be shared by faculty and students. One of these assumptions is that if God's existence were disproved, then religious commitment would have been shown to be unreasonable. Various religions, however, reject the notion of a supernatural God. These include Jainism, Theravada Buddhism, Mimamsa and Samkhya Hinduism, as well as Reconstructing and Humanistic Judaism in addition to *Death of God* versions of Christianity. Students should be made aware, therefore, that to be religious does not require belief in a supernatural God.

Here, for example, was how Rabbi Mordecai M. Kaplan, an opponent of supernaturalism, responded to a skeptic who asked why, if the Bible isn't taken literally, Jews should nevertheless observe the Sabbath:

> We observe the Sabbath not so much because of the account of its origin in Genesis, as because of the role it has come to play in the spiritual life of our People and of mankind . . . The Sabbath day sanctifies our life by what it contributes to making us truly human and helping us transcend those instincts and passions that are part of our heritage from the sub-human.[1]

And here is an account of the Holy Communion from one of the major figures in the Christian *Death of God* movement, John A. T. Robinson, the Anglican Bishop of Woolwich, who denied the existence of a God "up there" or "out there":

> [T]oo often . . . it ceases to be the holy meal, and becomes a religious service in which we turn our backs on the common and the community and in individualistic devotion go to make our communion with God "out there." This is the essence of the religious perversion, when worship becomes a realm into which to withdraw from the world to "be with God"—even if it is only to receive strength to go back into it. In this case the entire realm of the non-religious (in other words 'life') is relegated to the profane.[2]

Of course, a naturalistic religion can also be developed without deriving it from a supernatural religion. Consider, for example, the outlook of Charles Frankel, another opponent of supernaturalism, who nevertheless believed that religion, shorn of irrationality, can make a distinctive contribution to human life, providing deliverance from vanity, triumph over meanness, and endurance in the face of tragedy. As he put it, "It seems to me not impossible that a religion could draw the genuine and passionate adherence of its members while it claimed nothing more than to be poetry in

1. Mordecai M. Kaplan, *Religion Without Supernaturalism* (New York: Reconstructionist Press, 1958), 115–116.

2. John A. T. Robinson, *Honest to God* (Philadelphia: Westminster, 1963), 86–87.

which [people] might participate and from which they might draw strength and light."[3]

Such naturalistic options are philosophically respectable. Whether to choose any of them is for each person to decide.

Students should also recognize that theism does not imply religious commitment. After all, even if someone believes that one or more of the proofs for God's existence is sound, the question remains whether to join a religion and, if so, which one. The proofs contain not a clue. Indeed, God may oppose all religious practice. Perhaps God does not wish to be prayed to, worshipped, or adored, and might even reward those who shun such activities.

Yet another misleading assumption is implicit in the definitions that students are usually offered: a theist believes in God, an atheist disbelieves in God, and an agnostic neither believes nor disbelieves in God. Notice that the only hypothesis being considered is the existence of God as traditionally conceived; no other supernatural alternatives are taken seriously. But why not?

Suppose, for example, the world is the scene of a struggle between God and the Demon. Both are powerful, but neither is omnipotent. When events go well, God's benevolence is ascendant; when events go badly, the Demon's malevolence is ascendant. Is this doctrine, historically associated with Zoroastrianism and Manichaeism, unnecessarily complex and therefore to be rejected? No, for even though, in one sense, it is more complex than monotheism, involving two supernatural beings rather than one, in another sense, it is simpler because it leaves no aspect of the world beyond human understanding. After all, theism faces the problem of evil, while dualistic hypotheses have no difficulty accounting for both good and evil.

In sum, I would suggest that students should be reminded of the following four essential points: (1) Belief in the existence of God is not a necessary condition for religious commitment. (2) Belief in the existence of God is not a sufficient condition for religious commitment. (3) The existence of God is not the only

3. Charles Frankel, *The Love of Anxiety, and Other Essays* (New York: Harper & Row, 1965), 192.

supernatural hypothesis worth serious discussion. (4) A successful defense of traditional theism requires not only that it be more plausible than atheism or agnosticism but also that it be more plausible than all other supernatural alternatives. I am not suggesting, of course, that the proofs for the existence of God or the problem of evil not be taught. I am urging, however, that students be alerted to the limited implications of that discussion.

The one lengthy historical book in philosophy of religion found at least in abbreviated form in almost every introductory anthology is Hume's *Dialogues Concerning Natural Religion*. Yet because the main points of this masterpiece can be elusive, let me offer a few suggestions on guiding students in approaching the work.

Natural religion was the term used by eighteenth-century writers to refer to theological tenets provable by reason without appeal to revelation. The three participants in the *Dialogues* are distinguished by their views concerning the scope and limits of reason. Cleanthes claims he can present arguments that demonstrate the truth of traditional Christian theology. Demea is committed to that theology but does not believe empirical evidence can provide any defense for his faith. Philo doubts that reason yields conclusive results in any field of inquiry and is especially critical of theological dogmatism. Readers might anticipate that because Demea and Cleanthes are both theists, their positions will be mutually supportive. Matters, however, are not so simple, and students need to be alerted to the sophisticated interplay among the characters.

Remember that the *Dialogues* is a work of fiction, an account offered by one literary character, Pamphilus, to another, Hermippus, of a discussion Pamphilus claims he heard one summer day at the house of his teacher Cleanthes. As in any sophisticated drama, we are not simply told the point, we are shown it.

Some lessons, however, are obvious. The most widely used arguments for the existence of God are subjected to trenchant criticisms. In particular, the claim that the structure of the world provides clear evidence of God's handiwork, the so-called "teleological argument," is shown to be problematic.

Hume, however, not only undermines arguments for the existence of God but also develops in detail what is perhaps the strongest argument against the existence of God, namely, the problem of evil: How can evil exist in a world created by an all-good, all-powerful God? No glib dismissal of this perplexity can survive a careful reading of Hume's work.

But more is going on in the *Dialogues* than an examination of arguments for and against the existence of God. Indeed, the three central characters agree that "the question can never be concerning the being but only the nature of the Deity" (2, 3).[4] Yet how can we make sense of the view that something exists if all its attributes are unknown? Thus, the initial agreement among Cleanthes, Demea, and Philo that God exists is of dubious significance unless they come to some understanding of God's nature.

They struggle to do so, however, and if the traditional arguments for the existence of God have been shown to afford no understanding of the Divine, and the problem of evil forces the believer to seek refuge in God's incomprehensibility, theism is in danger of losing its meaning. I would propose this claim as the underlying theme of the *Dialogues*.

Hume's mastery is demonstrated in the development of this motif, for by subtle and realistic interplay among his three main characters, he brings to light the surprising affinity between the skeptic and the person of faith, as well as the lack of affinity between the person of faith and the philosophical theist.

For example, at the opening of Part 2, Demea states that God's nature is "altogether incomprehensible and unknown to us" (2,1). Philo agrees and speaks of "the adorably mysterious and incomprehensible nature of the Supreme Being" (2,4). Cleanthes, however, recognizes that these views may render theism vacuous, and so he launches into a statement of the teleological argument, thereby attempting to provide some understanding of the ways of

4. David Hume, *Dialogues Concerning Natural Religion and Other Writings*, ed. Dorothy Coleman (New York: Cambridge University Press, 2002). All references are to part and paragraph number.

God. Cleanthes's conclusion is that "the Author of nature is somewhat similar to the mind of man" (3,5).

But when Philo criticizes Cleanthes's analogy, Demea, who is suspicious of any attempt to describe the Supreme Being, sides with Philo, arguing that "the infirmities of our nature do not permit us to reach any ideas which in the least correspond to the ineffable sublimity of the Divine attributes" (3,13). Cleanthes warns Demea that if he persists in maintaining that God is wholly unknowable, he threatens to rob theism of any sense, but, with Philo's encouragement, Demea continues to defend his position.

In Part 10, where the discussion turns to the evils in the world, Cleanthes again finds himself opposing Philo and Demea, both of whom defend the view that "the whole earth . . . is cursed and polluted" (10, 8).

Cleanthes realizes that Philo can utilize the ills of the world to cast doubt on the existence of a God who is all-good and all-powerful, but Demea fails to appreciate this difficulty, confident that present evils will be rectified at some other time and place.

Cleanthes, however, is appalled by this line of reasoning because he believes that it amounts to nothing more than trying to explain away the damaging evidence of evil by appeal to an arbitrary supposition about an unknown afterlife. Cleanthes understands, as Demea does not, that taking a leap of faith in the face of strong evidence to the contrary raises doubts about the meaningfulness of one's faith.

Cleanthes attempts to defend the goodness of the world, hoping thereby to bolster the theistic position he and Demea share. But Philo, using evidence in part originally supplied by Demea, easily overwhelms Cleanthes, and Demea finally realizes that his apparent ally through much of the discussion has all along been his most dangerous enemy.

In Part 12, after Demea has become upset and departed, Philo tries to assuage his displeased host, Cleanthes. Many commentators have found this section puzzling because Philo proceeds to agree with Cleanthes that the universe exhibits purpose. The reader should have been aware by this point, though, that Philo's apparently theistic utterances are not all they seem to be, and Philo soon reveals the ambiguity of his admission.

In the end he adopts the view that the whole of natural religion is reducible to one proposition: "*That the cause or causes of order in the universe probably bear some remote analogy to human intelligence*" (12, 33). Yet because the import of this statement is undermined by such qualifications as "cause or causes," "probably," and "remote analogy," the claim is arguably neither theistic nor atheistic but simply unclear. We are left with Philo's observation that the proposition "affords no inference that affects human life . . . " (12, 33).

In the final sentence of the book, we are told that "Philo's principles are more probable than Demea's, but that those of Cleanthes approach still nearer to the truth" (12, 34). Those who assume this conclusion to be Hume's find it perplexing because so many of Cleanthes's arguments have been opposed throughout the work. The statement, however, is not Hume's but that of the narrator Pamphilus, who, as a student of Cleanthes, understandably finds Cleanthes's position the most persuasive of the three.

Why should Hume have ended the *Dialogues* with a misleading assessment of the discussion? A major part of the answer is that eighteenth-century English society took a dim view of attacks on traditional theological tenets. Because Hume had no desire to precipitate a scandal, he adopted the literary device of a narrator who at both the beginning and the end assures suspicious readers that, regardless of what might appear to have happened in the Dialogues, theism is triumphant.

Indeed, Hume's friends were so fearful of the public's disapproval that, despite his precautions, they dissuaded him from publishing the manuscript. Fortunately, he took pains to assure the work would not be lost, and it appeared in print three years after his death, although without any publisher's name attached.

Never before or since has traditional Christian theology faced a more dangerous philosophical attack. Whether it can be plausibly defended is a matter that students need to decide for themselves.

15

Teaching Ethics

When an introductory course arrives at the study of ethics, students are apt to embrace, without recognizing any of the associated difficulties, simplistic forms of subjectivism—i.e., moral truth varies from individual to individual, relativism—i.e., moral truth varies from culture to culture, egoism—i.e., people are motivated only by self-interest, or divine command theory—i.e., morality represents the will of God. Explaining these views and pointing out the problems they raise is an effective starting point. But the question then arises: If no easy answer will do, how can we reason about morality?

Some students will be prepared to believe that just as we are subject to scientific laws, such as water freezes at zero degrees centigrade and boils at one hundred degrees centigrade, so murder is wrong and honesty is right. Moreover, just as laws of nature apply at any time and place, so do moral laws. The only difference is that laws of nature are tested by scientific method, while moral laws are tested by conscience.

This theory, however, runs into troubles that other students will quickly point out. First, moral laws can be broken, whereas scientific laws cannot. A person can steal a book, thereby breaking a moral law, but cannot succeed in tossing a book into the air and prevent its being subject to the law of gravity. Second, the dictates of one person's conscience may conflict with those of another. How can we decide between them? We can appeal to the dictates of our own conscience, but ours may be biased. Or we can appeal to the dictates of the conscience of the majority, but theirs may also be mistaken. After all, moral principles are not decided by vote.

Perhaps, then, moral judgments aren't true or false but merely express preferences, thus leading back to subjectivism or relativism. Yet students need to be reminded that faced with social injustice they recognize its unfairness and may argue or demonstrate against it, seeking to change other people's minds. So, reasoning does appear to play a role in arriving at conclusions about right and wrong.

Given this impasse, how to proceed? One approach often overlooked is to consider the nature of moral judgments by first examining value claims unrelated to ethics. For instance, we speak of "a good restaurant" or "bad weather." How are these statements justified?

Here is the opportunity to work through a specific example. I've had success using sports, but some may find that other cases work as well or better. One of my favorite hypotheticals is to imagine that you are a member of a softball league. Your friend Beth tells you that Susan is an excellent ballplayer, so you ask her to join your team, but she turns out to be woefully inadequate. She drops balls thrown to her, fumbles ground balls, and strikes out almost every time she comes to bat. You tell Beth that her recommendation of Susan was a mistake. Either Beth does not know how to judge a good ballplayer or someone has misled her about Susan's abilities.

Notice that when you say that Susan is not a good ballplayer, you are neither appealing to the dictates of conscience nor expressing an arbitrary preference. Rather, you are basing your judgment on the facts—facts about softball, not facts about goodness. The reason Susan is not a good ballplayer are that she hits poorly and fields inadequately. To defend your view, you need only point to Susan's batting and fielding averages. Disagreement may persist if Susan hits .250 and commits a few errors, Without doubt, though, a ballplayer who hits .150 and commits errors in every game is not a good ballplayer, whereas one who hits .350 and rarely commits an error is a good ballplayer. The distinction is clear, despite the possibility of borderline cases, just as the distinction between bald and hirsute is clear despite the possibility of disputable instances.

Furthermore, if Susan hits and fields well, someone would be confused to wonder if Susan might still lack one attribute essential to a good ballplayer, namely, goodness, because if Susan hits and fields well, then she is a good ballplayer. Goodness is not another attribute besides hitting and fielding well but a shorthand way of referring to those skills.

Suppose when you tell Beth that Susan is not a good ballplayer, Beth agrees that Susan doesn't hit or field well, but argues that a good ballplayer is obliging to fans.

While Beth's reply would be exasperating, you could respond by emphasizing that the criteria of a good ballplayer are not arbitrary. You play softball to win; hence, good players are those who help in winning. Susan doesn't do so and thus is not a good ballplayer.

If Beth thinks players who are obliging to fans help the team win, her view can be disproven by an appeal to the record books. But if Beth believes softball is played not to win but to gain popularity, then players who are obliging to fans may be more effective in achieving that aim. In that case, however, Beth's recommendations of ballplayers would be of no value to the overwhelming number of participants whose aim in playing the game is to score more runs than the opposition.

We have extended this example far enough to clarify the nature of non-moral value judgments. First, although the term *good* is a term of commendation, the criteria for its use vary depending on the context and our purposes. Good apples, good computers, and good ballplayers are *good* for different reasons. Second, if two people disagree about a value judgment but agree on the criteria for goodness, then the disagreement is in principle resolvable with empirical testing procedures. Third, if the two people disagree about a value judgment and also disagree on the criteria for goodness, then the individuals need to consider why they have chosen their differing criteria. If a basis can be found for agreement on further ends that are supposed to justify the criteria, then the disagreement is again in principle resolvable with empirical testing procedures. If, however, the ends are fundamentally incompatible, then the disagreement will not yield to rational resolution.

Students will raise an obvious question: What are the chances that in a moral disagreement the disputants will agree on ends? At first glance, searching for consensus might appear hopeless, but it may be found by recognizing that we depend on others to achieve our most valuable goals. As Jonathan Harrison observed:

> We cannot conceive of a being like ourselves, who desires his own happiness, and the happiness of his family and friends (if not the happiness of the whole of mankind), who needs the company of his fellows, who is easily injured by their hostile acts, and who cannot continue to exist unless they co-operate with him—we cannot conceive of a being such as this approving of promise-breaking, dishonesty, and deliberate callousness to the interests of others."[1]

In short, our humanity requires that we rely on others, and therefore, we approve of actions that facilitate cooperation.

Any individual who rejects this way of thinking and instead favors persecution and cruelty for their own sake is not to be argued with but to be guarded against. Interestingly, no political leader has ever come to power by promising to increase hatred, violence, and oppression. To gain public support, even the worst of dictators mouths the usual moral sentiments.

Thus, if a moral skeptic should inquire why we should be concerned about the welfare of others, we can do no better than offer the response James Rachels provided: "The reason one ought not to do actions that would hurt other people is: other people would be hurt. The reason one ought to do actions that would benefit other people is: other people would be benefitted." If such

1. Jonathan Harrison, "Empiricism in Ethics," *The Philosophical Quarterly* 2:9 (1952).306.

considerations count for nothing, then the discussion is over. But what if someone insistently maintains a position in favor of immorality? Then, quoting Rachels again,

> [H]e is saying something quite extraordinary. He is saying that he has no affection for friends or family, that he never feels pity or compassion, that he is the sort of person who can look on scenes of human misery with complete indifference, so long as he is not the one suffering. . . . Indeed, a man without any sympathy would scarcely be recognizable as a man."[2]

The result is that a commitment to immorality is unlikely to be defended by anyone except an obstinate student in a philosophy seminar who nevertheless expects to receive kind treatment and an equitable grade, never noticing that these reflect a concern for ethical treatment.

One method of motivating students is to suggest a situation in which the available alternatives pose a conceptual challenge. Such a perplexity in the moral realm that has attracted much attention from contemporary ethical theorists is the trolley problem: Why do most people regard as acceptable the act of turning a trolley onto a spur so that one individual is killed rather than five, but regard as unacceptable pushing a large person over a railing so as to force a trolley onto a spur and kill one rather than five?

When students are presented with the case, they may respond that the various scenarios are implausible. After all, who has ever been in a position to shove a bulky man over a railing and thereby save the lives of workers on a track below? For that reason, such philosophical speculation may appear idle. To counteract that misconception, you might relate a story told by a survivor of the Shoah that, while serving as a reminder of its horrors, also illustrates why thinking about the role of a bystander as a tram approaches can illuminate how we should act in the face of unmitigated evil.

Near the end of World War II, prisoners in one concentration camp were sent on what was later termed a death march to avoid

2. "Egoism and Moral Skepticism," in Cahn, 380–389.

their being liberated. As they struggled to keep moving in a snowstorm, a Nazi guard handed a heavy bag to a prisoner and ordered him to carry it. The prisoner opened the bag, found food, ate some, and distributed the remainder to others. Upon seeing what had happened, the guard halted the march and sought to punish the offender. Due, however, to the snow and the similar clothing worn by all the prisoners, the Nazi was unable to determine who had opened the bag. He shouted that the perpetrator should identify himself, but when no one did, the guard announced that if the guilty party did not confess, every tenth prisoner would be shot. As this punishment was about to be carried out, one prisoner stepped forward and accepted responsibility. He was immediately killed, then the march continued. To this day, no one knows whether the prisoner who took the blame was the guilty party or instead had sacrificed himself to save the lives of numerous others.

Now vary the facts slightly. Suppose one prisoner took it upon himself to save many lives by choosing another prisoner at random and declaring that person guilty. Would the bystander's action of sacrificing one to save many have been morally wrong? Would your answer be the same if the bystander could have chosen to sacrifice himself but instead sacrificed someone else?

Notice that this version of the problem introduces a crucial complication, for the choice is not simply whether to sacrifice one to save others but to choose which single individual, including oneself, to sacrifice. In that case, the decision becomes far more problematic. Indeed, it adds weight to Judith Jarvis Thomson's view that unless you would be willing yourself to pay the cost of your good deed, you are not entitled to make someone else pay it. As she put it, "Of how many of us is it true that if we could permissibly save five only by killing ourselves, then we would? Very few . . . Then very few of us could decently regard ourselves as entitled to choose . . . saving the five but killing the one."[3]

In sum, while a trolley is for most of us a quaint image, and hypotheticals about altering its possible path may appear fanciful,

3. Judith Jarvis Thomson, "Turning the Trolley," *Philosophy & Public Affairs* 36:4 (2008), 366.

this version of the problem demonstrates that the underlying moral dilemma is potentially heartrending and all too realistic.

16

Teaching Political Philosophy

As students become familiar with philosophical inquiry, they realize that it tests widely held fundamental beliefs. The importance of doing so was stressed by John Stuart Mill, who wrote that "if the received opinion be not only true, but the whole truth; unless it is suffered to be, and actually is, vigorously and earnestly contested, it will, by most of those who receive it, be held in the manner of a prejudice, with little comprehension or feeling of its rational grounds."[1]

In our society, the received opinion in the political arena is the superiority of democracy over all other systems. To keep that view from turning into a mere prejudice, however, it needs to be challenged, and I know of no work that does so more effectively than Plato's *Republic.* While that remarkable book offers a unified account of central issues in metaphysics, epistemology, philosophy of mind, ethics, social philosophy, philosophy of art, and philosophy of education, the work makes as powerful a case as any against democracy, thus providing students with an inviting gateway into the study of the political realm.

Before introducing Plato, though, you might ask students to consider the following scenario. You go to a polling place on

1. Mill, 83.

election day. There, waiting to cast ballots, are the various members of the community—a carpenter, a gardener, a lawyer, a bus driver, a piano tuner, and an artist. Each has one vote, and the will of the majority prevails.

Standing in line, we might imagine, is Archie Bunker, the engaging but ill-informed and bigoted figure in the classic television sitcom *All in the Family*. Were Archie asked about his preferences, he might reply that he has no idea who is running in this election, but it makes no difference to him because he has voted for the same party his entire life and has no intention of ever switching. As for the bond issue that appears in the upper right-hand corner of the voting machine, he hadn't realized it was there, but now that you've mentioned it, he'll be sure to vote against it because he is against all proposed changes to the established system. (If Archie strikes students as a caricature, you might remind them that politicians always seek to place their names at the top of the ballot because a sizable number of voters select whichever name is first, apparently believing that higher is better.)

Standing behind Archie is a professor of political science who has devoted her life to an intense study of the American political system. She may be familiar with the views of every candidate and even have helped formulate the exact wording of the bond issue. Yet, like Archie, she receives only one vote; her erudition entitles her to nothing more.

Does this system make sense? After all, if you visit a physician seeking advice as to whether to undergo an operation, you would be appalled if the doctor explained that the policy in that office was to poll a random sample of passersby and act in accordance with the will of the majority. A community would be similarly dismayed if it hired an engineer to build a bridge, and the engineer announced that deciding how deeply to lay the foundations would be decided by a vote of the townspeople. In short, to deal with medical or engineering problems, we seek expert judgment, not the uninformed opinions of the populace. Why, then, faced with political problems, do we take the issue to all the people rather than to specialists?

Here you can introduce Plato, pointing out that he considered this same question. Believing no answer to be reasonable, he proceeded to construct a system of government based on the view that issues of political policy, being complex, technical matters, ought to be placed in the hands of experts. The Platonic utopia, therefore, was to be ruled by a small group of philosopher-kings, chosen on the basis of their aptitudes and educated for their roles. Most members of society were to be tradespeople: the farmer was expected only to farm, the cobbler only to cobble. They were to play no role in the governance of the state, and their education was to be in the narrowest sense a trade education.

Indeed, from Plato's viewpoint, to suggest that farmers or cobblers should participate in the affairs of government would be a grave mistake, for the farmer was fitted only to farm, the cobbler fitted only to cobble. The philosopher-kings were fitted to rule, and they would do so most effectively if not interfered with by those ill-suited to deliberate about decisions affecting the future of their society.

You might then remind students that Plato compared the workings of a democratic society to the situation aboard a ship on which the sailors are arguing over the control of the helm, while none has ever learned navigation. If someone on board happens to possess the needed skills, that person's qualifications will be disregarded on the grounds that steering a ship requires no special competence. Plato scornfully observed that "with a magnificent indifference to the sort of life a man has led before he enters politics . . . [a democracy] will promote to honor anyone who merely calls himself the people's friend."[2]

To ensure that those who serve as philosopher-kings are qualified to take on their responsibilities, Plato required that prospective officeholders embark on a rigorous intellectual program, topped off by the study of dialectic, that is, the study of explicating key concepts in the light of a vision of the good. No doubt many today would be more inclined to concentrate such advanced

2. *The Republic of Plato*, trans. Francis MacDonald Cornford (New York: Oxford University Press, 1945), 558c.

education for political leadership less on the intricacies of abstract reasoning and more on issues in political science, economics, sociology, and international relations. The force of Plato's proposal, however, is not found in the specifics of the curriculum he proposed but in the notion that officeholders should receive intellectual preparation for their positions.

Do students agree with this idea? Do they favor government by experts? Or would they agree with the late conservative writer William F. Buckley, Jr., who remarked, "I should sooner live in a society governed by the first two thousand names in the Boston telephone directory than in a society governed by the two thousand faculty members of Harvard University."[3]

These questions are likely to lead students to engage in spirited discussion about the strengths and weaknesses of the democratic system. Those skeptical about democracy might be reminded that, by whatever procedures the rulers of an oligarchy are selected, mistakes are possible, as the events of history have so often demonstrated. Once unrestrained authority is placed in the wrong hands, the results are likely to be calamitous. In a democracy, a foolish decision made on one occasion can be undone on another, but when all control has been transferred to the oligarchs, second chances are no longer possible. Members of a democracy avoid having to make an unalterable decision of whom to entrust with unrestricted power.

Furthermore, even if the rulers are initially kindhearted, in time they tend to lose touch with the ruled. Even the best-intentioned of sovereigns struggle to remain sensitive to the needs and desires of those under their control.

Although oligarchs may possess greater expertise in certain technical matters than do other individuals, members of a society possess special insight into their own problems, interests, and goals. As John Dewey pointed out, "The individuals of the submerged mass may not be very wise. But there is one thing they are wiser about than anybody else can be, and that is where the

3. *Rumbles Left and Right* (New York: Macfadden-Bartell Corporation), 1964), 103.

shoe pinches, the troubles they suffer from."[4] Only the democratic system ensures that this self-knowledge is taken into account in the governmental process.

A democratic society, moreover, is distinguished by the quality of life inherent in its procedures. Competitive elections require the expression of opposing points of view, and the protection of the right of all citizens to speak freely, write freely, and assemble freely, thus producing a vitality that enriches all.

For such reasons, Winston Churchill suggested that democracy is the worst form of government except for all the others that have been tried. Would Plato have been sympathetic to this claim?

Students will be surprised to learn that the answer is yes, but he expressed that view not in *The Republic* but in what is widely thought to be a later dialogue, namely, *The Statesman*. There, near the end of the work, Plato compares three types of government: monarchy, the rule of one; aristocracy, the rule of a few; and democracy, the rule of all.

Plato maintained that if the monarch is ideal, possessing moral and intellectual insight and treating all persons fairly, then monarchy is the best form of government. But if the monarch does not govern wisely, then monarchy can degenerate into tyranny, the worst form of government. Similarly, if a small group of rulers always governs wisely, then aristocracy is the second-best form of government. But if the aristocracy does not govern wisely, then it can generate into oligarchy, the second-worst form of government.

According to Plato, the advantage of democracy is that while it is capable of no great good, neither does it produce any serious evil. Thus, in a society like ours that is not perfectly law-abiding and in which all do not carry out their responsibilities appropriately, the best form of government, according to Plato, is democracy. Despite its faults, it poses the fewest dangers and is thus the wisest choice.

The case for democracy can thus be supported and Plato credited with a deeper understanding of the realities of politics than his critics often suppose. Nevertheless, his critique of democracy

4. Cahn, 552.

warns that a system that depends on the wisdom of the people is ever in danger of their making foolish choices that may lead to unexpected evils.

Political philosophy also includes the study of contemporary political problems, and for over fifty years, an especially divisive one has been affirmative action. Discussing it calmly and carefully would serve as a model for how reason can be applied to addressing contentious issues.

A promising start is distinguishing between procedural and preferential affirmative action. The former means taking steps to ensure that individuals are judged without considering their race, gender, or ethnicity. Doing so calls for openly announcing positions, banning biased tests unrelated to performance, and eliminating from all procedures any policies that harbor prejudice, however vestigial. Doing so is widely accepted as appropriate and does not give rise to controversy.

The source of the debate, however, is preferential affirmative action, which involves making special efforts to recruit individuals who meet institutional goals related to racial, gender, or ethnic identity. Advance any program of this sort, and the subsequent debate will generate more heat than light.

Part of the problem is that advocates of preferential affirmative action, which I shall henceforth refer to simply as "affirmative action," do not share one rationale. Is the aim to offset past discrimination, counteract present unfairness, or achieve future equality? The first is often referred to as "compensation," the second as "a level playing field," and the third as "diversity."

Note that each of these can be defended independently of the others. Compensation for past wrongs may be owed, although at present the playing field is level, and diversity is not sought. Or the present playing field may not be level, although compensation for past wrongs is not owed, and future diversity is not sought. Or future diversity may be sought, although compensation for past wrongs is not owed and presently the planning field is level.

Perhaps all three factors might be relevant, but each requires a different justification and calls for a different remedy. In particular, past wrongs would be offset if suitable compensation was provided, but once given to the appropriate recipients, no other steps would be needed. Present wrongs would be corrected if actions were taken to level the playing field, but doing so would be consistent with unequal outcomes. Future equality would require continuing attention to ensure that an appropriate balance, once achieved, would never be lost. Defenders of affirmative action would likely favor at least one of these policies but not necessarily more than one. The matter needs clarification.

Nowadays, the most frequently cited defense of affirmative action is an appeal to diversity. That term, however, requires a modifier, such as racial diversity, gender diversity, religious diversity, and so on. Without this clarification, the usefulness of the concept of unmodified diversity comes into question.

To see why, imagine a ten-person philosophy department that has no African American, no woman, no person under forty, no non-Christian, no registered Republican, none who served in a war, none who is gay, none who was ever on welfare, none who is physically challenged, none whose work is outside the analytic tradition, and none who specializes in aesthetics. When the next appointment is made, which characteristics should be stressed so as to render this department more diverse? I know of no compelling answer, but an appeal to diversity requires one.

To put the matter more vividly, suppose that the finalists for a position in that department include an African American, a woman, a thirty-year-old, a Buddhist, a Republican, a veteran, someone who was once on welfare, someone who uses a wheelchair, a gay person, a specialist in continental philosophy, and an aesthetician. Whom does diversity favor? The answer is unclear.

Note that different considerations may arise in justifying affirmative action in student admissions. After all, colleges traditionally take into account a high school applicant's athletic prowess, community service, personal relationships to alumni, and geographic home. Such criteria, however, are not considered in a faculty search. No wonder defenders of affirmative action are most comfortable supporting it in the context of a complex admissions decision involving many non-academic factors, while opponents most often think of the policy in relation to assessing the research and teaching of applicants for faculty positions. The two decisions are different in kind, and the same arguments may not apply to both.

In addition, circumstances matter. Consider a department that has never appointed a woman and, when given a promising opportunity, refuses even to grant an interview. Suppose the dean insists that in the next search process, highly qualified women should be interviewed, and if a woman with a superlative record is found, she should be appointed. Would opponents of affirmative action object? I think not.

On the other hand, consider a department that announces its intention to achieve a goal of fifty percent women, and, in the following search, prefers a minimally qualified woman to a man who is far more promising as a researcher, teacher, and contributor to the life of the department. If the dean insists that the man be appointed, would proponents of affirmative action be upset? Again, I think not.

Both these cases are admittedly extreme, although not entirely unrealistic, but the lesson is that presuming affirmative action to be at odds with merit, as its opponents do, or to be a means of obtaining justice, as its defenders do, are oversimplifications. The context matters.

In sum, this discussion of a disputed matter has clarified relevant issues but left conclusions open, thereby allowing students to develop their own positions. As explained earlier, such is the appropriate way to teach philosophy.

17

Improving Teaching

When we write a paper, we typically show a draft to at least one of our colleagues. We find someone whose judgment we trust and who offers criticism in a constructive spirit. Then we share our work and almost always benefit.

Why not follow the same procedure with teaching? Find a sympathetic soul who takes teaching seriously and show that person a draft of your syllabus. Then adjust it in accord with any reactions you find helpful.

Furthermore, once the course begins, invite that individual to attend a session and share thoughts on the proceedings. The observer should sit in the back of the room and refrain from taking any role, as participation impedes disinterested evaluation. Afterwards, with the benefit of the observer's perspective, you should discuss all aspects of the session: how well a question was formulated, how discussion may have gone off the track, whether you were audible, whether your writing on the chalkboard was visible, whether your PowerPoint slides were helpful, how a difficult concept might have been presented more clearly, or how an idea explained in one context might have been applied in another. The aim is not to interfere with your distinctive teaching style but to enhance it.

Three major pitfalls should always be of concern:

1. Did you neglect to interest students in the subject by not connecting the course material with the students' own experiences?
2. Did you confuse students by either assuming background knowledge they lacked or proceeding too quickly for them to follow the reasoning?
3. Did you trivialize the positions of your intellectual opponents, failing to explain clearly why they disagree with you?

Of course, if you believe for any reason that someone lacks the know-how or willingness to offer helpful remarks, don't invite that person. Just as you would not ask for help on a paper from someone ill-suited to the task, the same is true for requesting feedback on teaching.

Yet why would someone agree to spend time and effort to attend your class, then sit with you afterwards to provide a review? Because you will offer to do the same in return.

Such exchange visits are not formal observations intended to serve as part of a promotion or tenure review. Rather, they are informal arrangements meant to benefit both you and your colleague. Admittedly, you may not agree with every suggestion offered, but almost surely you will learn something of value from the reactions of an informed observer who brings to your efforts a different perspective.

I recognize that many instructors object to the presence in their classes of colleagues, but almost all faculty members welcome auditors, friends or relatives of students, and even faculty members from other departments. Why, then, be reluctant to invite a knowledgeable and sympathetic commentator who can offer useful advice?

Granted, this practice is not a panacea. More often than not, though, it will be productive and may on occasion prove revelatory.

18

A Teacher's Mission

About three decades ago, I served on the jury in a highly publicized, double-murder case. The defendant was a mother who was charged with killing her two newborns and attempting to kill her third. In court, she admitted the crimes but pleaded insanity. The trial took several weeks, with dueling psychologists offering conflicting testimony. At the end, the jury was sequestered during its two days of deliberation, and eventually the defendant was found not guilty by reason of mental disease or defect.

While I still recall many of the details, what I remember most vividly is the seriousness with which the jury carried out its responsibilities. From the moment we entered the courtroom and saw the accused sitting with her lawyer at the defendant's table, the weight of the moment affected us deeply. The other jurors and I listened carefully to the judge's instructions and made every effort to carry out our duties as scrupulously as possible. A woman's life hung in the balance, and our responsibility was to ensure that justice was done. After the verdict was announced, we were pleased when several officers of the court came to the jury room to thank us for our service and indicate that they believed we had reached an appropriate decision.

Most importantly, although we were forced to endure a variety of inconveniences, we realized that the proceedings had not been planned to suit us. We were being asked to make a momentous judgment and were expected to do so as conscientiously as possible, regardless of our personal preferences about the process.

Let me now contrast this experience with an occasion many years before when my brother and I took a cruise to Nassau. From the moment our ship left the dock until the time we returned, the crew made every effort to cater to our wishes. Food and drink were available at our request, and innumerable activities were arranged for our pleasure. We were the focus of attention, and the aim of the enterprise was to fulfill as many of our wishes as possible. Of course, the hope was that we would find the experience a positive one and register for additional cruises. Although I never did because I found the rocking of the ship to be unsettling, I admit that having one's expressed desires fulfilled without delay by an amiable crew is delightful.

Now I ask: As a faculty member, do you expect the experience to be more like serving on a jury or taking a cruise? In other words, do you expect administrators and colleagues to seek every opportunity to satisfy your desires, or do you anticipate that the obligation to guide students and treat them fairly will weigh on your conscience and temper your enjoyment?

For example, suppose you are asked to share office space when you would prefer to have your own. Or you are given a Monday, Wednesday, Friday schedule, although you would rather not teach on Fridays. Or you are asked to offer a course that is not your first or second choice.

If you are expecting to be a passenger on an academic cruise, then you will be greatly upset by these inconveniences. But if you think of yourself as a member of an academic jury, then these matters will assume far less importance. After all, as a juror, the room in which you meet may be cramped and windowless. The court's schedule may be inconvenient, and you may spend hours waiting for the trial to proceed. You will be required to forgo reading any newspapers or watching any media that might contain relevant stories. You may even be sequestered for a time, cut off from home and family. Yet a person's life or welfare may hang in the balance, and thus you put aside every annoyance and concentrate, instead, on fulfilling the duties you have been sworn to uphold.

As a teacher, you also assume serious responsibilities, and, although you may rarely think of the matter in these terms, your actions may put students at risk. Which of us has not been victimized by an instructor's meanness or carelessness? Or been blinded to some potentially fascinating subject by an incompetent, tedious, or aberrant presentation?

Granted, teachers are not usually in position to impact an individual's life to the extent a jury might, but the activities of professors can influence the future of society, strengthening or weakening its members' skills in thinking, interpretation, and evaluation.

Thus, joining a faculty is far closer to serving on a jury than taking a cruise, for we owe the community our every effort to replace ignorance and prejudice with understanding and reason. Such is a teacher's mission, and we should be prepared to take pains and shoulder burdens in trying to fulfill it.

Works by Steven M. Cahn

BOOKS AUTHORED

Fate, Logic, and Time
Yale University Press, 1967
Ridgeview Publishing Company, 1982
Wipf and Stock Publishers, 2004

A New Introduction to Philosophy
Harper & Row, 1971
University Press of America 1986
Wipf and Stock Publishers, 2004

The Eclipse of Excellence: A Critique of American Higher Education
(Foreword by Charles Frankel)
Public Affairs Press, 1973
Wipf and Stock Publishers, 2004

Education and the Democratic Ideal
Nelson-Hall Company, 1979
Wipf and Stock Publishers, 2004

Saints and Scamps: Ethics in Academia
Rowman & Littlefield, 1986
Revised Edition, 1994
25th Anniversary Edition, 2011
(Foreword by Thomas H. Powell)

Philosophical Explorations: Freedom, God, and Goodness
Prometheus Books, 1989

Puzzles & Perplexities: Collected Essays
Rowman & Littlefield, 2002
Second Edition, 2007

God, Reason, and Religion
Thomson/Wadsworth, 2006

From Student to Scholar: A Candid Guide to Becoming a Professor
(Foreword by Catharine R. Stimpson)
Columbia University Press, 2008
Second Edition, Wipf and Stock Publishers, 2024

Polishing Your Prose: How to Turn First Drafts Into Finished Work
(with Victor L. Cahn)
(Foreword by Mary Ann Caws)
Columbia University Press, 2013

Happiness and Goodness: Philosophical Reflections on Living Well
(with Christine Vitrano)
(Foreword by Robert B. Talisse)
Columbia University Press, 2015

Religion Within Reason
Columbia University Press, 2017
Second Edition, Wipf and Stock Publishers, 2025

Teaching Philosophy: A Guide
Routledge, 2018

Inside Academia: Professors, Politics, and Policies
Rutgers University Press, 2019

The Road Traveled and Other Essays
Wipf and Stock Publishers, 2019

Philosophical Adventures
Broadview Press, 2019

A Philosopher's Journey: Essays from Six Decades
Wipf and Stock Publishers, 2020

Philosophical Debates
Wipf and Stock Publishers, 2021

Navigating Academic Life: How the System Works
Routledge, 2021

Professors as Teachers
Wipf and Stock Publishers, 2022

Exploring Academic Ethics
Wipf and Stock Publishers, 2024

Pathways Through Academia
Wipf and Stock Publishers, 2025

Towards Teaching Philosophy
Wipf and Stock Publishers, 2026

BOOKS EDITED

Philosophy of Art and Aesthetics: From Plato to Wittgenstein
(with Frank A. Tillman)
Harper & Row, 1969

The Philosophical Foundations of Education
Harper & Row, 1970

Philosophy of Religion
Harper & Row, 1970

Classics of Western Philosophy
Hackett Publishing Company, 1977
Second Edition, 1985
Third Edition, 1990
Fourth Edition, 1995
Fifth Edition, 1999
Sixth Edition, 2003
Seventh Edition, 2007
Eighth Edition, 2012

New Studies in the Philosophy of John Dewey
University Press of New England, 1977

Scholars Who Teach: The Art of College Teaching
Nelson-Hall Company, 1978
Wipf and Stock Publishers, 2004

Contemporary Philosophy of Religion
(with David Shatz)
Oxford University Press, 1982

Reason at Work: Introductory Readings in Philosophy
(with Patricia Kitcher and George Sher)
Harcourt Brace Jovanovich, 1984
Second Edition, 1990
Third Edition (also with Peter J. Markie), 1995

Morality, Responsibility, and the University: Studies in Academic Ethics
Temple University Press, 1990

Affirmative Action and the University: A Philosophical Inquiry
Temple University Press, 1993

Twentieth-Century Ethical Theory
(with Joram G. Haber)
Prentice Hall, 1995

The Affirmative Action Debate
Routledge, 1995
Second Edition, 2002

Classics of Modern Political Theory: Machiavelli to Mill
Oxford University Press, 1997

Classic and Contemporary Readings in the Philosophy of Education
McGraw Hill, 1997
Second Edition, Oxford University Press, 2012

Ethics: History, Theory, and Contemporary Issues
(with Peter Markie)
Oxford University Press, 1998
Second Edition, 2002
Third Edition, 2006
Fourth Edition, 2009
Fifth Edition, 2012
Sixth Edition, 2015
Seventh Edition, 2020

Exploring Philosophy: An Introductory Anthology
Oxford University Press, 2000
Second Edition, 2005
Third Edition, 2009
Fourth Edition, 2012
Fifth Edition, 2015
Sixth Edition, 2018
Seventh Edition, 2021
Eighth Edition, 2024

Classics of Political and Moral Philosophy
Oxford University Press, 2002
Second Edition, 2012

Questions About God: Today's Philosophers Ponder the Divine
(with David Shatz)
Oxford University Press, 2002

Morality and Public Policy
(with Tziporah Kasachkoff)
Prentice Hall, 2003

Knowledge and Reality
(with Maureen Eckert and Robert Buckley)
Prentice Hall, 2003

Philosophy for the 21st Century: A Comprehensive Reader
Oxford University Press, 2003

Ten Essential Texts in the Philosophy of Religion
Oxford University Press, 2005

Political Philosophy: The Essential Texts
Oxford University Press, 2005
Second Edition, 2011
Third Edition, 2015
Fourth Edition, 2022

Philosophical Horizons: Introductory Readings
(with Maureen Eckert)
Thomson/Wadsworth, 2006
Second Edition, 2012

Aesthetics: A Comprehensive Anthology
(with Aaron Meskin)
Blackwell, 2008
Second Edition (with Stephanie Ross and Sandra Shapshay), 2020

Happiness: Classic and Contemporary Readings
(with Christine Vitrano)
Oxford University Press, 2008

The Meaning of Life, 3rd Edition: A Reader
(with E. M. Klemke)
Oxford University Press, 2008
Fourth Edition, 2018

Seven Masterpieces of Philosophy
Pearson Longman, 2008

The Elements of Philosophy: Readings from Past and Present
(with Tamar Szabó Gendler and Susanna Siegel)
Oxford University Press, 2008

Exploring Philosophy of Religion: An Introductory Anthology
Oxford University Press, 2009
Second Edition, 2016

Exploring Ethics: An Introductory Anthology
Oxford University Press, 2009
Second Edition, 2011
Third Edition, 2014
Fourth Edition, 2017
Fifth Edition, 2020
Sixth Edition, 2023

Philosophy of Education: The Essential Texts
Routledge, 2009

Political Problems
(with Robert B. Talisse)
Prentice Hall, 2011

Thinking About Logic: Classic Essays
(with Robert B. Talisse and Scott F. Aikin)
Westview Press, 2011

Fate, Time, and Language: An Essay on Free Will by David Foster Wallace
(with Maureen Eckert)
Columbia University Press, 2011

Moral Problems in Higher Education
Temple University Press, 2011
Wipf and Stock Publishers, 2021

Political Philosophy in the Twenty-First Century
(with Robert B. Talisse)
Westview Press, 2013

Portraits of American Philosophy
Rowman & Littlefield, 2013

Reason and Religions: Philosophy Looks at the World's Religious Beliefs
Wadsworth/Cengage Learning, 2014

Freedom and the Self: Essays on the Philosophy of David Foster Wallace
(with Maureen Eckert)
Columbia University Press, 2015

The World of Philosophy
Oxford University Press, 2016
Second Edition, 2019

Principles of Moral Philosophy: Classic and Contemporary Approaches
(with Andrew T. Forcehimes)
Oxford University Press, 2017

Foundations of Moral Philosophy: Readings in Metaethics
(with Andrew T. Forcehimes)
Oxford University Press, 2017

Exploring Moral Problems: An Introductory Anthology
(with Andrew T. Forcehimes)
Oxford University Press, 2018

Philosophers in the Classroom: Essays on Teaching
(with Alexandra Bradner and Andrew Mills)
Hackett Publishing Company, 2018

An Annotated Kant: Groundwork for the Metaphysics of Morals
Rowman & Littlefield, 2020

The Democracy Reader: From Classical to Contemporary Philosophy
(with Andrew T. Forcehimes and Robert B. Talisse)
Rowman & Littlefield, 2021

Academic Ethics Today: Problems, Policies, and Perspectives on University Life
Rowman & Littlefield, 2022

Privacy
(with Carissa Véliz)
Wiley-Blackwell, 2023

Understanding Kant's Groundwork
Hackett Publishing Company, 2023

Bronx Socrates: Portrait of a Legendary Teacher
Wipf and Stock Publishers, 2024

About the Author

STEVEN M. CAHN is Professor Emeritus of Philosophy at the City University of New York Graduate Center, where he served for nearly a decade as Provost and Vice President for Academic Affairs, then as Acting President.

He was born in Springfield, Massachusetts, in 1942. His early years were devoted to music, and he studied piano with Herbert Stessin of the Juilliard School and the noted chamber music artist Artur Balsam. He also became a professional organist under the tutelage of the eminent composer Isadore Freed.

After earning an AB from Columbia College in 1963 and PhD in philosophy from Columbia University in 1966, Dr. Cahn taught at Dartmouth College, Vassar College, New York University, the University of Rochester, and the University of Vermont, where he chaired the Department of Philosophy and led the successful effort to build what remains one of the country's most highly rated undergraduate programs.

He served as a program officer at the Exxon Education Foundation, as Acting Director for Humanities at the Rockefeller Foundation, and as the first Director of General Programs at the National Endowment for the Humanities. He formerly chaired the American Philosophical Association's Committee on the Teaching of Philosophy, was the Association's delegate to the American Council of Learned Societies, and was longtime President of the John Dewey Foundation, where he proposed and brought to fruition the John Dewey Lectures, now delivered at every national meeting of the American Philosophical Association.

He has presented numerous addresses at colleges and universities throughout the United States, including the first Naumberg Memorial Lecture at UCLA, the Minerva Lecture at Union College, the convocation address at Florida International University, and a keynote speech to the Kenan Convocation at the University of North Carolina at Chapel Hill. He has also spoken at meetings of numerous organizations, including the College Entrance Examination Board, the American Board of Internal Medicine, the American Association of State Colleges and Universities, the National Association of Academic Affairs Administrators, and both the Northeastern and Midwestern Association of Graduate Schools.

He is the author of more than twenty books and editor of over fifty others. He has also served as general editor of four multivolume series: *Blackwell Philosophy Guides, Blackwell Readings in Philosophy, Issues in Academic Ethics,* and *Critical Essays on the Classics.*

His numerous articles have appeared in a broad spectrum of publications, including *The Journal of Philosophy*, *The Chronicle of Higher Education*, *Shakespeare Newsletter*, *The American Journal of Medicine*, *The New Republic*, and *The New York Times*.

A collection of essays written in his honor, edited by two of his former doctoral students, Robert B. Talisse of Vanderbilt University and Maureen Eckert of the University of Massachusetts Dartmouth, is titled *A Teacher's Life: Essays for Steven M. Cahn* (Wipf and Stock Publishers). His professional autobiography appears in his book *The Road Traveled and Other Essays.*

Index

INDEX

www.ingramcontent.com/pod-product-compliance
Lightning Source LLC
LaVergne TN
LVHW020647100826
845148LV00012B/2362

* 9 7 9 8 3 8 5 2 6 1 2 6 0 *